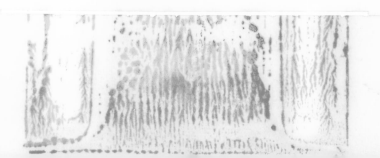

VOLLEYBALL

ROBERT E. LAVEAGA

**Formerly, Professor of Physical Education
Springfield College**

SECOND EDITION

THE RONALD PRESS COMPANY • NEW YORK

3

Library of Congress Catalog Card Number: 60-14603
PRINTED IN THE UNITED STATES OF AMERICA

Preface

There have been so many changes and developments in the game of volleyball since the previous edition of this book that this revision is a complete rewrite. With the acceptance of volleyball as one of the Olympic sports and its inclusion in the last two Pan-American Games, volleyball has come into full recognition internationally. This step into world competition brings with it a greater emphasis on what is known as power volleyball.

This book sets forth this style of play for championship volleyball, but it also discusses thoroughly a second type known as recreational volleyball, in which the players are not training for championships but are playing for fun and exercise. The author feels that the general rules and techniques should be observed in this game, too.

Fundamental techniques of the pass, serve, attack, and blocking are presented with illustrations. Defensive and offensive play is discussed for both the intensive and the recreational game, and suggestions for advanced styles of play are given in the chapter on training for competition. The chapter on volleyball for girls and women calls attention to the recent developments on merging rules with those for men. Since many girls play a modified volleyball, consideration is given to the modified game, and to advanced play as well.

Volleyball is now recognized as one of the leading activities in the total sports program of schools, clubs, and teacher training agencies. Consequently a general syllabus is outlined for the presentation of the game along with coaching suggestions and hints on developing interest in class and intramural play. Chapters on the fundamentals of officiating, on equipment, and on the background of the game round out the book.

The author is grateful for the rewarding fellowship with the leaders of the United States Volleyball Association and for the many materials published in its Annual Guide; for the important articles on the game appearing over the years in *The Journal of Physical Education;* for the continuous information and insight on the game presented in *The International Volleyball Review;* for the opportunity to teach and coach the game at Springfield College and for the encouragement and help of Dr. Ellis Champlin, Professor Fred Geisler, and Mr. V. Hubert Dhanaraj.

Teamwork is necessary for winning volleyball; likewise, teamwork on the home front made this book possible. Words cannot express the appreciation which the writer has for the loyal support of his wife, Priscilla, and for her helpful work in illustrating the text.

Robert E. Laveaga

Belmont, Mass.

August, 1960

Contents

1. History of the Game 3

2. Fundamentals and Principles 8

3. Techniques of Handling the Ball 13

4. Serving the Ball 31

5. The Attack 44

6. Defensive Play 57

7. Offensive Play 69

8. Training for Intensive Competition 79

9. Officiating 91

10. Equipment 103

11. Volleyball for Girls and Women 111

12. Class Organization 120

Index 127

VOLLEYBALL

1

History of the Game

The game of volleyball was invented in 1895 by William G. Morgan, at that time the physical director of the Holyoke, Mass., YMCA. He had large classes of businessmen and felt that a game was needed which would provide an opportunity for their recreation and relaxation. Basketball seemed suited to younger men, but there was a need for something not quite so rough and strenuous for the older men. In looking for a suitable game, Mr. Morgan considered tennis, but this required rackets and other equipment and so it was discarded, although the idea of using a net was retained. Mr. Morgan raised a tennis net to a height of 6 feet, over which a basketball bladder was volleyed. However, this proved to be too light and slow. A basketball was then tried, but this was too large and too heavy. General specifications for a volleyball were then proposed and submitted to A. G. Spalding and Brothers. The resulting ball, which was smaller and lighter than a basketball, met with approval.

Soon afterward, the game (then known as Mintonette) was demonstrated by two teams from Holyoke before a group of YMCA physical directors who were attending a conference held at Springfield College in Springfield, Mass.

The game met with their immediate approval, with the exception of its original name, "Mintonette." Dr. Luther H. Gulick of the college faculty suggested that another name be found. Dr. Alfred T. Halstead, also of the Springfield College faculty, noted that the nature of play, i.e., "volleying the ball," suggested the name "Volley Ball," which was accepted.

The first article on this new game appeared in the YMCA publication *Physical Training* in the July, 1896, issue. It was written by J. Y. Cameron of the Buffalo (New York) YMCA. In this article the following comment was made:

> Volleyball is a new game which is pre-eminently fitted for the gymnasium or the exercise hall, but which may be played out of doors. Any number of persons may play the game. The play consists in keeping the ball in motion over a high net from one side to the other, thus partaking of the character of the two games, tennis and handball.

3

EARLY RULES OF THE GAME

The following rules, taken from the same article, offer some interesting sidelights on how the game was played in its beginning days:

1. **Game.**   The game shall consist of nine innings.
2. **Innings.**   An inning consists of:
   a. When one person is playing on each side, one service on each side.
   b. When three or more are playing on each side, three serves on each side. The man serving continues to do so until out by failure of his side to return the ball. Each man shall serve in turn.
3. **Court.**   Twenty-five feet wide by fifty feet long.
4. **Net.**   Two feet wide and twenty-seven feet long. Top of net six feet six inches from the floor.
5. **Ball.**   The ball shall be a rubber bladder covered with leather or canvas. It shall measure not less than twenty-five inches nor more than twenty-seven inches in circumference, and shall weigh not less than nine ounces nor more than twelve ounces.
6. **Server and Service.**   The server shall stand with one foot on the back line. The ball must be batted with the hand. Two services or trials are allowed him to place the ball in the opponents' court, as in tennis. In a service, the ball must be batted at least ten feet, no dribbling allowed. A service which would strike the net, but is struck by another of the same side before striking the net, if it goes over into the opponents' court, is good. If it goes outside, the server has no second trial.
7. **Scoring.**   Each good serve unreturned or ball in play unreturned by the side receiving, counts one score for the side serving. A side only scores when serving, as a failure to return the ball on their part results in the server being put out.
8. **Net Ball.**   Ball hitting net, aside from the first serve, is counted as a dead ball.
9. **Line Ball.**   Counted out.
10. **Play and Players.**   Any number of players. Touching the net by players puts the ball out of play. Holding the ball is banned. Ball hitting any object out of the court and bounding back into the court is counted as a good ball. Dribbling is allowed within four feet of the net.

The game developed rapidly under the supervision of the YMCA Physical Directors' Society. The following changes in rules were made in 1900: *game,* 21 points; *net,* 7 feet; *line ball* counted as in court; ball striking obstruction ruled out of court; *dribbling* prohibited.

In 1912 a special committee of YMCA men was assigned to the task of studying the rules. They recommended the following changes: *court,* 35 by 60 feet; *net height,* 7 feet 6 inches; *net width,* 3 feet; and the introduction of *rotation.*

In 1917, the first complete Volleyball Guide made its appearance, being published by the American Sports Publishing Company of New York. The National Collegiate Athletic Association joined with the YMCA in the preparation of the rules. Dr. George J. Fisher was editor of the Guide and held this position until 1950 when Marshal L. Walters of Springfield College assumed the editorship. Starting with the 1951 Guide, the Berne Witness Company of Berne, Indiana, has published the Guide.

DEVELOPMENT OF CHAMPIONSHIP COMPETITION

Intensive volleyball received added impetus when the YMCA promoted its own National Championship in 1922 at the Brooklyn Central (New York) YMCA. Twenty-seven teams from eleven states battled for the first title. Three Pennsylvania teams—Pittsburgh, Germantown, and Johnstown —finished first, second, and third in that order. The championships proved to be a great stimulus in the progress and improvement of the game.

Volleyball took another forward step when in 1922–23 the National Athletic Federation adopted the YMCA and Collegiate Rules, and the Rules Committee was made a subcommittee of the Federation. In 1925 the Army, the Navy, and the Women's Division of the National Amateur Athletic Federation were added to the agencies participating in the framing of the rules. In 1926 the rules were printed in the Red Cover Series of the Spalding Athletic Library, with a special section on rules for women and girls. More changes were made in the rules from the period 1922 to 1926 than during any preceding period.

In 1928 two significant events took place, namely, the organization of the United States Volleyball Association and the announcement that the National YMCA Championships would be made open championships. Dr. George J. Fisher was made president of the United States Volleyball Association. He gave 24 years of stimulating leadership to volleyball, and his retirement in May, 1952, brought to a conclusion an inspiring, active, and dedicated service to the game.

With the formation of the United States Volleyball Association, many organizations joined forces for the advancement of the game. At the present time the following organizations are members of the Association (USVBA):

American Association for Health, Physical Education and Recreation
American Latvian Association
American Turners
Armed Forces
Boys' Clubs of America
Boy Scouts of America
National Amateur Athletic Union
National Collegiate Athletic Association

National Council of YMCA's
National Jewish Welfare Board
National Recreation Association
Physical Education Society of the YMCA's of North America
Society of State Directors of Health, Physical Education and Recreation
Representatives of U.S. Volleyball Association Players

The United States Volleyball Association meets in the spring in conjunction with the championships. Changes in rules are considered at this time. A second meeting is held in December at the location of the forthcoming championships. At the present time there are the following divisions in the championships: Open, YMCA, Women's, Collegiate, Armed Forces, and YMCA Masters (formerly the Veterans, 35 and over).

Schools and colleges have come to recognize volleyball as an important activity for their recreation and physical education programs. In 1949 an Intercollegiate Division was included in the championship series.

Volleyball is now an established sport in the Pan-American Games. In the 1955 games held at Mexico City, the game was enthusiastically received. All tickets were sold out before the games opened. Terrific smashes, brilliant blocking, and sensational fielding characterized the play. In these games the United States defeated the Mexican team for the men's championships, and in the women's division, Mexico defeated the team from the United States. In the 1959 games at Chicago the United States men's team was again victorious against Brazil, Mexico, Dominican Republic, Venezuela, Canada, Puerto Rico, Cuba, and Haiti, who finished in that order. The Brazilian women's team defeated the United States, with Peru and Puerto Rico trailing.

Volleyball is now listed among the Olympic sports, and the games to be held in Tokyo in 1964 will undoubtedly include volleyball. This favorable action took place at the 1957 meeting of the International Olympic Committee when it approved volleyball as one of the 21 approved sports.

There are 40 or more countries that now belong to the International Volleyball Federation with headquarters in Paris, France. This body holds world championships every four years, the fourth World Championships being held in Brazil in 1960. The Federation has been an important factor in attaining Olympic recognition of the sport, which has grown rapidly in favor in world-wide competition, attracting immense crowds in Europe, Africa, the Latin American countries, and particularly in countries behind the "Iron curtain" and in the Orient. International tours have been encouraged and taken by teams from other countries as well as the United States.

Supporting this international emphasis has been a quarterly magazine devoted to volleyball. Starting in 1940 as a mimeographed *National Volleyball Review,* it blossomed into print in November, 1947, as the *International Volleyball Review.* The editor is Harry Wilson of Hollywood, California.

This magazine brings information on the game and the results of play around the world.

The game has steadily developed in style of play over the years, from a "seesaw," slow moving one to a spectacle of exciting, vigorous action. The service has passed through several stages, from a slow lob to an effective, offensive weapon. The passing has steadily developed to the point that there is a clean-cut handling of the ball. Strict officiating has been responsible for this development, since the majority of officials penalize low passes which are made with the open hand, palms-up position. The one- and two-hand closed-fist pass has been substituted for the scooping type of play.

The block has increased and intensified the work of the attack. Rules permitting unlimited blocking by all members of the team have forced the spikers to do more than smash the ball straight away into the opponents' court. Recovering blocks has become one of the features of the game. General defensive play has improved, and many "impossible shots" have been successfully recovered.

Volleyball has developed in a remarkable style. Physical education training institutions now offer training courses in volleyball. As a result of better teaching in the grades, high schools, and colleges, volleyball is rapidly becoming an accepted and popular activity. The armed forces include volleyball in their program and conduct intramural as well as world championships. And in addition, the game is a favorite at camps, on playgrounds, and with many organizations promoting a recreational program. Volleyball has come a long way since 1895 when William Morgan hung a tennis net across the Holyoke "Y" gym and volleyed a basketball bladder back and forth.

2

Fundamentals and Principles

The game of volleyball is similar to the game of tennis in that a ball is played back and forth over a net. Each team attempts to make the ball hit the opponents' court, and likewise, each team endeavors to keep the ball from doing so. This must be done without touching or going over the net or center line. Points are scored by the serving team when the receiving team fails to play the ball properly and return it over the net.

TYPES OF VOLLEYBALL PLAY

It should be recognized that there are two distinct types of the game, the recreational and the highly competitive. With the recreational game, play may range from a happy-go-lucky, ball-banging style, where good fellowship and fun are the main objectives, to well-organized team play. This is the type of game we find in camps, on playgrounds, and in gymnasium classes. The intensive type of team play is known today as *power volleyball*. This game calls for exciting action and requires considerable training. It is a flashy, hard-driving, fighting game which commands the best of condition and highly developed individual and team skills. Our National and International Championships are exhibitions of this kind of play.

In the early development of volleyball, the recreational game was played universally. When the championships were initiated in 1922, the game increased in intensity, calling for advanced skills. New systems of play were instituted, and improved tactics and strategy became a part of good team play. The training of a modern volleyball team demands as much practice and conditioning as other major games of today.

COURT AND TEAM REGULATIONS

The official USVBA rules govern play for women and girls as well as for men, the only difference being the height of the net. For women it is 7 feet 4¼ inches instead of 8 feet.

COURT DIMENSIONS.   The outside dimensions of the court are 60 by 30 feet (see Diagram 1).   This area is divided across the center by a net 3 feet wide, the top of which is 8 feet from the floor.   There is a center line 2 inches in width across the court under the net.   In addition there is a spiking line for back-field players, across the court which is parallel to and 7½ feet from the center line.   The measurements for this line are taken from the center points of both lines.

NUMBER OF PLAYERS.   A volleyball team has six players, three of whom start play in the front of the court and three in the rear.   Their positions have designated names in relation to the court (see Diagram 1).   These are: left forward, center forward, right forward, right back, center back, and left back.   The rules require that when the ball is served, each of these players must be in his respective position.   The forward players must be in front of the back-line players, and there should be no overlapping of feet forward or sideward.   As soon as the ball is served, players may move to any part of the court, the only restriction being that of prohibiting back-line players from spiking the ball in front of the spikers' restraining line.

BEGINNING INSTRUCTION.   In teaching the game to beginners, divide the six players into three pairs.   This is known as the 3–3 system; one player of the pair is called the *set-up* and the other the *spiker,* or the *attack.*   The set-up player is responsible for the recovery and placement of the ball so that the spiker can hit it over the net into the opponents' court.

For convenience in explaining the game, let us use the letter A to designate one team and B the other.   The winner of the coin toss, team A, starts the game by making the first serve.   The player in the right-back position goes to the serving area, which is directly in back of the end line.   He may serve from any point in back of this line.

Serving the Ball.   All other players must be in their respective positions. After the ball has been hit in the serve, all players, including the server, may move from their positions to any place on the court.   The service is made by hitting the ball with the hand, fist, or arm into the opponents' court.   It must go over the net without touching it and land in the court.   If it goes out of bounds or hits an obstruction, the serve is lost, and no points are scored for either side.   If the serve is successful, team B plays the ball.

The first man to receive the ball is known as number 1.   It is his duty to pass the ball high into the forward part of the court near the net to number 2, in such a manner that he will be able to get under it.   Number 2 is known as the set-up, and his responsibility is to pass the ball high and close to the net so that the next player, number 3, will be able to jump in the air and hit the ball into the opponents' court.   This sequence is known as the 1–2–3 standard play in the 3–3 system.   Other formations will be dealt with in advanced play in later chapters.

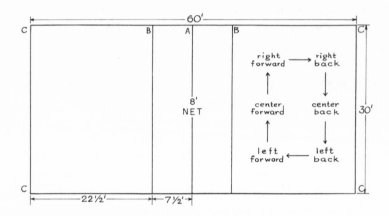

Diag. 1. Volleyball court showing dimensions and relative positions of players and rotation direction. (A) Center line. (B) Back-line players spiking line. (C) Serving area. Arrows indicate rotation direction.

RULES FOR SCORING. The rules specify that the ball may be played only three times on each side of the net. Players are not permitted to hit the ball twice in succession. However, number 1 could pass it to another player and then have it returned to him to be hit on the third play. Volleying continues back and forth until one side fails to return the ball or commits an error or foul. When team A is serving and team B fails to return the ball, or has a foul called on it, team A scores one point.

To win a game, a team must have a two-point advantage after having scored 15 points. If the score is 14 to 14, play continues until one team has a two-point advantage. Recently the rules have included the 8-minute time limit game. If one team has a two-point advantage at the end of 8 minutes of playing time, it is declared the winner. If it lacks a two-point advantage, play continues until one team has scored a two-point margin.

If team A fails to make a legal serve or fails to return the ball over the net during play, it loses the ball and no points are scored for either team. When the serving team forfeits or loses the ball, the opponents *rotate*, each player moving one position in a clockwise manner (see Diagram 1): right forward moves back to the serving area in back of the end line; the right back to the center-back position; the center back to the left back; the left back goes forward to the left forward position; the left forward to the center position; and the center forward moves to the right forward area.

THE REFEREE. The referee is the chief official of the game, and his position should be on a platform so constructed that he can have a clear vision of the top of the net and both courts. (See Chapter 9 for the more important rules that he enforces.)

STANDARD PLAY

The general principles of team play in the game of volleyball are quite simple. As previously mentioned, there are two lines of players, the front and the back, composed of three players each. When the ball is served, all the players must be in their respective positions. Back-line players are not permitted to spike the ball in front of the 7½ foot restraining line. They also carry major responsibility for recovering the ball and passing it forward to the set-up player.

In tournament play in the United States there is strict officiating in regard to how the ball is handled. The rules indicate that the ball must be hit and not thrown. The use of the double-underhand, palms-up pass is not permitted, and special attention is also given to the reception of power serves and hard-driven spikes. It is of great importance to teach beginners the clear-cut hitting action rather than anything which would approximate a held ball.

The teamwork of the three pairs is of great value, especially the pair at the net. In all offensive play, the strategy is to work the ball up to the net in such a position that the set-up will have an opportunity to get into the most favorable position to pass the ball to his spiker partner. If the pass comes up to the front of the court low and away from the set-up, the chance for proper play is minimized. In volleyball the passer or set-up player is like the guard in basketball or football. He does the less spectacular work, while the spikers are in the limelight. This is modified in modern play by having a greater number of spikers.

A fundamental principle of play is to play the ball three times rather than hit it over the net on the first or second play. The set-up rarely sends the ball over the net on the first or second play. The spiker tries to outwit the opposition by placing the ball in open spaces or by driving it through the defensive formation. The use of the block (defensive play at the net) intensifies the play of spikers and decreases their effectiveness.

There are standard plays in the game which make for efficiency. Diagrams 2 and 3 show two fundamental positions into which each team rotates (for right-handed spikers). The basic play is to pass the ball to the set-up whose attack (spiker) is on his left at the net. In the first instance the set-up is in the center-forward position, and in the second, in the right-forward position. In general it is an accepted principle that for beginning play, the

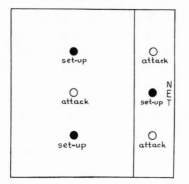   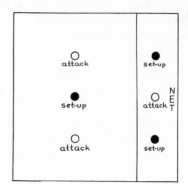

Diag. 2. Set-up attack combination.   Diag. 3. Reverse positions
                                                         of Diagram 2.

set-up always gets the second ball. This eliminates confusion and uncertainty and makes for smooth play.

When a team has mastered the 3–3 style of play, it is ready for the modern 4–2 play. In this system there are four spikers and two set-ups. Principles of this will be discussed in the chapter on offensive play.

The basic play is quite simple, but when two teams have practiced and have developed their skills and teamwork, the game can be a thrilling and delightful experience. Intricate serves, skillful recovering, precision setting-up, powerful spiking, and obstructive blocking go to make up a combination of team play that is most enjoyable for participants and spectators alike.

3

Techniques of Handling the Ball

Satisfactory and successful play in volleyball depends on the ability to handle the ball properly. One reason why ardent and enthusiastic beginners fail to stay with the game is their unwillingness to learn the simple fundamentals of proper finger, arm, and body coordination. The average novice should be able to learn these fundamentals in a comparatively short time. The teacher or coach should continually emphasize the importance of this skill and should encourage each player to take pride in his ability to handle the ball. However, it takes years of constant practice to become highly skilled.

In the recovery of a ball that has been played across the net by the opponents, the receiver plays the ball according to his relationship to it. A skilled performer has a keen sense of angles and forces which are present in playing the ball. This includes the speed that the ball is traveling and how much force it will take to counteract it. There are several factors involved in its recovery. First is the line of flight of the ball as it approaches; second, the direction to be given the ball for a satisfactory play; third, the angle of the recovery surface; and last, the line of applied force, which carries through the axis of the ball.

A fundamental principle in passing the ball is to play it whenever possible with what is known as the *chest* or *head pass*. That is, having the arms and hands raised in front of the chest or head. In this position one is able to play the ball with greater efficiency and risks less liability of being penalized for a held ball. If the ball is below the waist and to the side or in front of the body, it will be necessary to play the ball in an underhand manner, either with one or two closed fists, the back of the hand, or with the double, open hand. This latter method is not popular these days because of the strict rulings by officials. However, in recreational volleyball it is used regularly. Players entering tournament play should be prepared to have an error called on them if they use the double-underhand "palms-up" method of recovery.

Let us consider some of the fundamental techniques of handling the ball.

13

PLAYING THE LOW BALL

It has been indicated that some methods of playing a low ball are favored over others in view of the strictness in calling held balls. In the intensive game, if a player hits the ball with an up-turned hand or hands, he is immediately penalized for holding the ball. This development has forced coaches to substitute techniques that are acceptable, namely, the closed fist or fists, the back of the hand, the wrists or the forearms. In the development of team play, which is based on individual skills, ball handling is of paramount importance.

THE ONE-HAND UNDERHAND PASS.   This pass is recommended in place of the double underhand pass. It has had exceptional success in major tournaments and is known as a *dig* pass. With it, one is able to get under hard hit balls in difficult positions for remarkable recoveries. While control is difficult because of the limited surface of the closed fist, sufficient balls are recovered to make it a valuable play.

In fielding the ball, the body should be in a state of readiness, weight on the balls of the feet, and with knees slightly bent to allow straightening of the body at the instant of contact. The fingers are closed into a fist position with the thumb adjacent to the index finger, and the hand is rotated outward (see Diagram 4).

In this pass the solid surface of the fingers, thumb, and heel of the hand is placed in the path of the ball, and attention is given to hitting the ball squarely under the center and up through the ball. The blow with the closed fist is short and sharp, flexing both the wrist and the elbow when the ball reaches the hand. Effort should be made to control the ball and place it for the next play rather than to hit it with too much force. It should be kept in mind in the execution of this pass that the striking surface is placed in a position to intercept the ball squarely and then moved just enough to pass the ball to the desired spot. The ball rebounds easily and with little effort to the force applied directly to its center.

Some players use the back of the hand in a similar manner, placing the hand in a position to intercept the ball squarely, and giving a flip of the wrist to bounce the ball at contact. If the first two joints of the fingers are

Diag. 4. The one-hand underhand pass.

flexed and the third joint is held in line with the back of the hand, there will be a flat surface formed for playing the ball.

THE TWO-HAND UNDERHAND PASS (THE "DIG"). Modern volleyball experts are in agreement that the best method for recovering low-hit balls is with combinations of the closed hand, or both hands, wrists, and forearms. The two-hand *dig* method of recovery is now a fundamental tactic in the game. Here are two different placements of the hands, wrists, and forearms in recovering low balls:

In the first method one hand makes a fist and is grasped within the other hand with the thumbs on top, side by side (see Diagram 5). The elbows are moved inward to align the wrists and forearms side by side. The body crouches, with knees slightly bent. The hands, wrists, and forearms are placed low in a position to intercept the ball and are held at an angle which will cause the ball to be squarely struck and hit into the air. As the ball strikes the wrists and forearms, the knees and body are slightly straightened with an easy motion, calculated to give an upward bounce to the ball. This alignment is placed to intercept the ball, and the wrists roll upward through the ball for a distance of 8 or 10 inches. However, a hard-driven ball needs but little power from the contact.

THE RUSSIAN PASS (see Diagram 6). Secondly, information regarding another method of passing was given to the writer by V. Hubert Dhanaraj of Madras, India, who had observed Russian players using it in their play to recover low-hit balls. The two thumbs are placed against each other in alignment with the two index fingers, which meet in front of the thumbs and are pointed forward. The other fingers join in forming a steeple-like

Diag. 5. The two-hand underhand pass (the "dig").

Diag. 6. The Russian pass.

position. The index fingers should be spread, and the thumbs join at their tips in order to form a flat and rounded surface to play the ball. Other fingers also join likewise. This position is readily assumed and is reported to have given excellent results.

THE KICK PASS. The present rules permit the use of any part of the body in playing the ball. It is possible, therefore, for a player to use his feet, except in serving the ball. Players may put the kick pass to good use in defensive play, or in an emergency situation when a player is caught out of position or makes an extraordinary effort to recover the ball by using one or both feet. In general it is not advisable to overemphasize this possibility. It may cause careless play.

The ball may be played by the side of the foot or the instep. The instep may be formed into a more or less flat surface by depressing or extending the toes. The contact with the ball should be under its center, with a definitely controlled kick just powerful enough to lift it into the air for play by a team mate. A ball may also be recovered by placing one foot flat on the floor and letting the ball hit it. The ball should never be forcibly kicked as a football, in view of possible injuries.

THE DOUBLE UNDERHAND PASS (Palms up). The double underhand pass has been a fundamental play since the origin of the game in 1895. With the development of the highly competitive game, this style of handling the ball has been practically eliminated from major tournament play. However, as previously noted, there are many places where the underhand method is still in use. In many recreational and class programs this style is permitted, especially for those learning to play the game. This style of passing is not efficient, and every effort should be made to encourage a beginner to handle the ball properly. Recognizing the fact that the underhand method of passing is used by some volleyball groups, the following techniques of the underhand pass are presented (see Diagram 7).

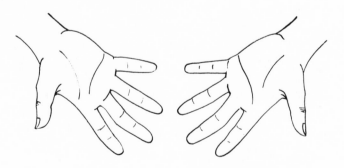

Diag. 7. The double underhand pass (palms up).

To execute the underhand pass, the feet are spread, with one foot slightly advanced and the knees bent. The arms are flexed at the elbows and rotated so that the thumbs are pointed outward. The palms are turned up, and the fingers are tensed, slightly spread, and pointing forward in front of the body. The body is bent forward in readiness for the oncoming ball.

The upward passing movement starts in the knees, body, and shoulders and is followed by the arm swing. The pass is executed by an upward swing in which the arms are raised and rotated outward as the fleshy parts of the fingers hit the ball in a forceful manner. At the moment of contact, the fingers, wrists, and arms are tense, and in the resulting action the ball is batted rather than lifted or held. The body, head, and shoulders straighten as the arms, wrists, and hands swing forcefully to the sides. It is of great importance that the fingers alone be the contact points. If the ball touches the palm of the hand, there is much greater chance that the ball will be held. In this pass, also avoid hitting the ball with the heel of the hand. Concentrate on hitting with the fleshy pads of the fingers.

PLAYING THE HIGH BALL: THE HEAD PASS

TECHNIQUES OF THE HEAD PASS. The best and surest method of handling a ball is with the head pass. In this pass, the ball is played in front of or above the head. In order to play the ball in this manner, it may be necessary for a player to move forward, to the side, backward, or sink to his knees in order to get under the ball. In a great majority of plays, it will be possible to recover and play a ball with this method of passing. Time spent in learning the fundamentals of this pass will yield rewarding results in playing ability. The beginner should be encouraged to utilize the head pass whenever possible. If he is permitted to use the underhand pass, it will impair his ability (Diagram 8).

If at first the initial movements seem awkward, the reason is that it is a new position to assume and a new action to learn. However, within a short

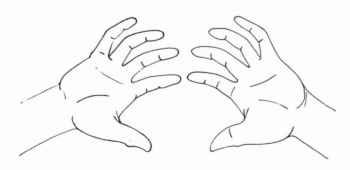

Diag. 8. The head pass.

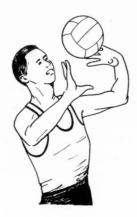

Diag. 9. Position prior to contact with ball.

period of instruction and practice, a beginner will sense an ability to control
the ball and the power to make a satisfactory pass.

In this movement the left foot is advanced in order to give a comfortable
stance. The knees are slightly bent and the body is tilted forward. The
elbows are flexed and raised sideward to a point in line with, or just below,
the shoulders. The wrists are extended and in line with the forearms; wrists
and hands are rotated inward. The extent of this rotation depends on the
length of the thumbs and fingers and the angle of the backward body bend
prior to hitting the ball. The hands are placed in front of the head, and
the thumbs point in toward each other and form the base of a triangle in
which the index fingers form the sides.

Some coaches advocate sighting the oncoming ball through this triangle.
The fingers are tense and spread and point toward the opposite hand (see
Diagram 9).

The position described above provides a concave surface, formed with the
fingers, palms, and heels of the hands. The volleyball should fit into this
pocket, which now resembles a bowl. Prior to the reception of the ball, the
up-and-down diameter of this surface is nearly vertical. In order to give the
feel of this position and the correct placement of the hands and arms, the
student should catch the ball and hold it in the correct position. Emphasis
should be made that the ball be played from the fleshy pads of the first joints
of the fingers and thumbs, making an instantaneous ten point contact. The
ball should not touch the palms of the hands. As a player holds the ball,
the teacher will have a splendid opportunity to note faulty positions in
stance, body, arms, wrists, and fingers. Although this exercise is a simple
one, it is important in learning the passing skill. Beginners should be
motivated to take serious concern in the value of the movement and to be

Diag. 10. Position of arms and hands in the follow-through.

made aware that holding the ball will be penalized by the referee in a regular game.

For greater accuracy, and to save time, toss the ball to a student rather than attempt to pass it to him. This toss should attain a height of approximately 12 feet and should drop down just in front of the student. Note that when the body bends backward or when the elbows are raised, the angle of the receiving surface of the hands changes from a vertical plane (assumed prior to the reception of the ball) to one in which the surface of the so-called bowl is tipped upward to meet the oncoming ball. The greater the back bend, the nearer the surface approaches the horizontal plane. The correct body bend, position of elbows, and arms and finger placement must be worked out to suit each individual player.

The next step is to have the student bat the ball instead of holding it. The teacher should demonstrate the correct pass, showing how easily the ball can be handled and controlled when the whole body coordinates in the movement. Emphasize the "elbows-out" position, the backward cocking of the wrists just before the ball is hit. Point attention to the forward roll of the fingers as the ball is hit with a full upward extension of the arms for power, which leaves the fingers pointing directly upward at the end of the pass (see Diagram 10).

Toss the ball to the beginner. As the ball starts its downward flight, coach the player to extend his hands slightly to meet it, following the ball back without touching it until it is at head height. At this point the fingers and wrists stiffen in contacting the ball, which is hit with ten points of the finger pads. This impact must be of a forceful clicking or flicking movement to avoid an error for holding the ball. The arms are extended upward at this time until they have reached the outstretched position. This extension gives power to the pass.

When making the pass the whole body comes into action. The knees are straightened, the body and shoulders come forward, and the weight is shifted from the back to the front leg as the arms, wrists, and fingers are fully extended. There is a sense of accomplishment and pride in the attainment of this simple passing skill.

WEAKNESSES OF THE BEGINNER. Be on the alert for the following weaknesses which the beginner usually has:

1. The elbows are dropped, which means that the fingers are pointing upward. This position results in a slapping action that decreases control of the ball.
2. The fingers are slightly flexed and curled in, making for a poor receiving surface.
3. The fingers are relaxed and placed together. (The correct position for the fingers is to have them pointing in toward each other, spread out and tense.)
4. The ball touches the palm of the hand. It will go dead.
5. Failure to get under the ball.
6. Failure to get full extension of the body, arms, and hands.
7. Failure to hit the ball correctly, by making successive contacts rather than the advised ten-point hit.

COACHING POINTS IN TEACHING THE HEAD PASS

1. Position of Elbows. Beginners have a tendency to lower their elbows when playing the ball. Previous experience in basketball has conditioned many players to drop the elbows. When this happens, you will note that the fingers are pointed upward and the heels of the hand project forward. The resulting action is a slapping motion by the hands or a direct hit by the heels of the hand. Neither of these is efficient. When the elbows are raised to shoulder height, the fingers point in toward each other and the ball will be hit with all ten points, which gives much more control to the pass. Upward-pointed fingers may be injured more readily than when they are placed in the correct "pointed-in" position.

2. Getting Under the Ball. In order to make a good pass, it is necessary to get under the ball and to face in the direction in which the ball is to travel to the next player. Failure to do so forces a player to make a second-best pass. If power is lacking to get the ball to the required height or distance, look for the fault in the limited extension of the legs, body, arms, or hands. A player must follow through in making a proper pass. At times a player will relax his fingers, thereby weakening the pass. Teachers should be on the lookout for beginners who have a tendency to curl or flex their fingers.

3. Determining a Correct Pass. One method of determining whether the ball has been handled properly, especially by beginners, is to listen to the sound when the hands contact the ball. When all ten fingers hit simultaneously in a correct pass, there is a clicking sound. It is distinct and leaves little doubt as to the ball being hit properly. The sound is quite distinguishable from that heard when the ball visibly comes to rest in the hand or touches the palm or heel of the hand, for the sound of such play is a dull, thudding one. Players should understand what is meant by passing the ball with a "click" and not a "thud."

Another clue that will be helpful is to note the amount of spin which is imparted to the ball by the passer. If all ten points of the fingers hit the ball at the same instant, the ball will float. This is a good point to make. The greater the spin, the more likely that the novice is hitting the ball with successive contacts.

4. Placement of the Pass. The height of a good pass ranges between 15 to 20 feet. This gives the receiver an opportunity to get under the ball. In making a pass, beginners should learn to pass the ball so that it will come down in front of the next player. A regular fault of beginners is to pass the ball over and beyond the receiver. It is much easier to come forward and play a ball than to move backward for it. Practice is of paramount importance in learning how to hit and control the ball.

THE SET UP

Closely allied to the pass is the set up. In beginning volleyball, there are three regular set-up players to each team, who work with their respective spikers. It has been emphasized that each player must develop skill in handling the ball, but the set-up player is required to give special attention to recovering the ball and setting it up in such a manner that the spiker will be able to play it effectively.

The set-up player usually receives the second ball. If the pass is good, he should make an efficient set up, but there are times when he must travel some distance to get under the ball or must play a speedy low ball. These balls are difficult to handle and result in improper placement of the ball for the spiker. It is absolutely essential that the set-up use the head pass in the majority of plays. This method ensures a reliable control of the ball.

KINDS OF SET UPS. Generally speaking there are four kinds of set ups: the high, the low, the over-the-head, and the long-distance (Diagram 11).

The High Set Up. The first is the high set up, which is passed up into the air to a height of 15 or more feet. This is so placed that it will descend to a point within 6 inches to 3 feet from the net. Some tall rangy players like this type of set up and are able to play it effectively as far back as 6 to 10 feet from the net. In general it is better to have it passed close to the net. The high set up close to the net is losing favor in view of the effectiveness of the block.

The Low Set Up. The second type of set up is known as the low set up.

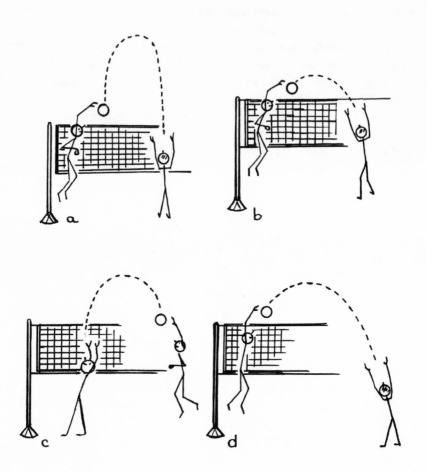

Diag. 11. Types of set ups.

This is passed 2 or 3 feet above the net and very close to it, 3 to 12 inches. This is effective in quick plays, especially when the defense is not able to get set for the play. This kind of set up is much easier for the spiker to hit, as the ball seems to "hang" in the air, thereby giving the attack player a better chance to hit. The low set up calls for expert timing on the part of the two players involved, as the ball may be hit on the way up, when it reaches its height, or when it is falling. In all cases the ball is moving at a comparatively slow speed. The set-up player should receive the ball when he is close to the net. The farther back from the net he is forced to play the ball, the more difficult will be the set up. This is a flashy, spectacular play that offers great possibilities.

Included in this section is the *medium arc set up,* which is played to either side of the court. The ball is set up to a height of 10 to 12 feet and calls for a quick reaction on the part of the spiker.

The Over-the-Head Set Up. The third set up is known as the over-the-head set up. This has received much attention during recent years, especially in tournament volleyball. This play occurs when the set-up is in the center position, with spikers on either side. The ball is passed to the set-up, who looks to be set for a pass to the spiker on his left side. All preliminary movements are the same as in the head pass except that, just before contact is made, the direction of the extended arms change to a backward movement, the head is tilted back, and the back is arched. The spiker on the right side, who has been given a signal, comes in and spikes the set up.

There will be other opportunities to play the ball in this manner, especially with the freedom of players to move into any position on the court. This play calls for careful teamwork. Well-coached teams have systems of signals to indicate when such plays are to be used.

The Long-Distance Set Up. The fourth type of set up is the long-distance set up. This play is made when the ball is set up from a point 10 feet or more back from the net. Instead of passing the ball high into the air, it is sent diagonally forward on a low arch to the net. This set up should be high enough to go over the net in case the spiker fails to hit it. A well-skilled team may use this kind of a pass on the first play rather than play the ball three times.

PLACEMENT OF THE SET UP. In setting up a ball, the height will vary from 10 feet for a low set up to 18 or more feet for a high set up. The correct height will depend on the requirements of the spiker. He should be

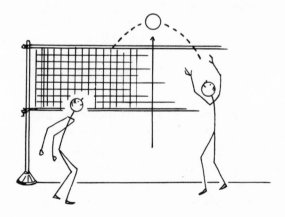

Diag. 12. Set up made in front of the attack.

vocal in letting the set-up players know where and how he wants the ball to be placed for his attack. This point may vary from 6 inches to 3 feet from the net. It should be kept in mind that the farther back from the net one is forced to hit the ball, the more limited will be the angle of placement. However, there are players who are skilled in hitting the ball when it is set up on or in back of the spikers' restraining line

In passing, the highest point that the ball reaches should be midway between the set up and the attack. Far too many set ups have been misplaced because they have been passed too far over the head of the spiker. To recover such balls, the spiker is forced to reach backward over his head. In this position he is off balance and his striking power is limited. Furthermore he is likely to be fouled for throwing or pushing the ball. The set-up should therefore make every effort to keep the ball in front of the attack. Sometimes the set-up passes the ball directly upward over his own head, then steps back and lets the spiker come in after the ball. This is helpful for players who have the fault of continually overcasting their set ups.(Diag.12).

It is also important to emphasize the position which the set-up takes when passing to the attack, namely, to face his spiking partner whenever possible. In some instances he will be forced to make a backward, over-the-head pass, but in general, he will be able to maneuver into the correct passing position, especially if he has faithfully practiced this skill.

In setting up balls which fall below the chest, the set-up should drop down on one or both knees and use the head pass. However, if the ball cannot be handled in this manner, the set-up may use the closed-hand method, i.e., using a single fist or hand, or the double underhand method of recovery.

PRACTICE SUGGESTIONS

Players who are really concerned about learning the art of passing correctly should be motivated to practice faithfully. Practice in passing skills will aid in the development of the muscles of the fingers and arms as well as improve the coordination of the entire body. The following suggestions will be useful in presenting passing fundamentals to beginners. Players with advanced skills will find these suggestions helpful also.

Practice 1. Form a circle 20 feet in diameter, players (five or six) facing the instructor or an advanced player standing in the center. The instructor tosses the ball to each in turn and has him pass it back to him. This will give the instructor an opportunity to spot weaknesses in the beginner's pass. Toss the ball so that it will drop down in front of the student. The height of the toss should be about 15 feet from the floor. If the student has to move an appreciable distance, especially backward, it will add to the difficulty of the pass. It may be necessary to toss the ball several times to the same person at the beginning of this practice. Before the actual passing practice begins, it would be well to have all players assume the correct position for making the head pass.

Toss the ball around the circle to each player in turn. Increase the height of the toss as players develop in skill. Encourage players to return the ball with a high pass. Emphasize getting under the ball and passing it up so that it will be in a good position for the next play.

Practice 2. In this exercise, use the same formation. Instead of tossing the ball from the center, the ball should be hit with the regular passing technique. All players will now practice hitting the ball with the head pass.

Practice 3. All players stand in circle formation. The ball is passed around the circle from player to player, first to the right and then to the left. In this exercise, great importance is made of two additional points: first, that in recovering the ball, the passer should face in the direction of the next player to receive the ball. Second, if the pass is being made to the right, the immediate player on the passer's right is held responsible for recovering the ball.

Practice 4. In a class situation it is well occasionally to add the recreational and competitive elements. Use the circle formations. Give each group a ball. On the signal to "go," each group will start passing the ball. The object is to see which group is able to make the greatest number of successive passes before the ball touches the floor. Each group counts audibly the number of successful passes. When the ball hits the floor, the group starts a new count.

At the beginning, players may use any type of pass and may hit the ball more than once in succession. As they develop, restrictions may be made as to the type of passes allowed for scoring.

Practice 5. Form two lines facing each other about 15 feet apart. Pass the ball back and forth and up and down the lines. The height of the pass should be about 12 to 15 feet. Increase the distance between the lines and also the height of the pass as players improve.

Practice 6. Three players face three others at the net. Pass the ball over the net, working for a controlled pass that just clears the net. Move back from the net for practice in distance passing.

Practice 7. Two players face each other close to the net. They use the net as a guide and pass the ball to each other, keeping the ball close to the net but not going over it.

Practice 8. Two players face each other about 10 feet apart, having a basketball goal between them. Pass the ball back and forth over the goal to each other.

Practice 9. Player A stands under a basketball or special volleyball goal.

Player B stands about 10 feet in front of the goal. A tosses the ball to B, who tries to pass it into the basket.

Practice 10. Two players stand beside a wall facing each other, about 15 feet apart. Pass the ball back and forth to a marked height on the wall.

Practice 11. A single player faces a wall. He practices passing the ball to the wall and recovering and passing it when it falls. It would be well to mark areas on the wall that can be used for regular practice. There is a passing test known as the Brady test which utilizes this arrangement (see page 28). This exercise is an excellent conditioner.

Practice 12. Form a 15-foot diameter circle. Practice hitting the ball with the closed fist. Caution the players to work for control in this pass. Forceful flexion of the wrist is to be avoided. Pass the ball around or across the circle. All players will have to be on the alert in view of the speed the ball travels at times.

Practice 13. Form a circle, using two balls for six men. Each player in turn passes the ball five times over his head, working for control, and then passes it on to the next player.

Practice 14. Players are in file formation. Leader of the line stands over a mark on the floor. He tosses the ball 12 feet above his own head, after which he turns to the right and goes to the end of his line. Number two in line advances and plays the ball as it falls, attempting to pass the ball over the mark on the floor. Each player moves up in turn and tries to pass the ball so that it will be near the original mark. With several groups this drill may be competitive, to see which group is nearest to its mark when time is called.

Practice 15. Line up two files facing each other, about 15 feet apart. One ball is given to the leader of one of the columns. He passes the ball across to the head of the opposite file and runs across to the right and joins the end of this opposite file. With rapid passing back and forth, this exercise is active and interesting.

Practice 16. Recovering the ball from the net. The instructor throws the ball into the net and players in turn recover it before it hits the floor. Players line up close to the net. To start, throw the ball into the lower quarter of the net. It will be noticed that with the swing of the net, the ball pauses in the air for a brief moment. However, when the ball hits higher on the net, you will note that it drops or springs off the net with greater speed. For practice, toss the ball into the lower net first and gradually work up.

Practice 17. Set up practice. Stretch a string across the court about 10 feet above the net and 12 inches back. Have a player A stand near the net. Player B passes the ball from the back court to A. A sets the ball up, aiming to touch the string.

Practice 18. Long pass drill. Player A stands in back of the end line of the court. B stands 20 feet in front of him. B tosses the ball to A at a 20-foot height. A attempts to hit the ball over the net. This drill is valuable for strengthening the fingers, wrists, and arms. A progressive exercise would be to have A bat the ball to B instead of tossing it to him.

Practice 19. Place six men on the court, in regular formation. Player A stands in the center of the opposite court, facing the net. A tosses the ball to each back-line player in turn. On the reception of the ball, it is passed forward to the set-up, who then sets it up for the spiker to hit. Rotate players after each of the back-field players have had a chance to make three passes. This is an excellent exercise to teach the principles of team play.

TESTS

Volleyball programs can be improved through the rating of players, for it will give information on their ability and effectiveness. Through tests, a teacher learns of the strengths and weaknesses of his pupils and is able to classify them. Unfortunately there is a definite lack of valid volleyball tests. It is necessary for volleyball teachers and coaches to utilize the tests that are now available or to formulate their own. If a player continually makes an error in handling the ball, it will show on the rating chart and can be pointed out to him. Such studies furnish an opportunity to establish norms for evaluating individual and team play.

The following skills may be used for grading players:

1. Toss ball into air and set it up a few feet overhead.
2. Toss ball into air and make a long, high pass.
3. Receive a softly hit ball and set it up overhead.
4. Receive a softly hit ball and make a long, high pass.
5. Toss ball into the net and recover.
6. Receive hard-hit or served ball and make high pass forward.
7. Receive hard-hit or served ball below the waist; use double closed fist to recover.
8. Receive and set up ball while standing near net.
9. Receive ball while standing near net and set it up backward over head.
10. One-hand fist recovery of low ball.
11. Recover blocked ball at net and set it up.

Rating a player while he is in action is a valuable asset in studying the abilities of individual players. While this technique is not necessarily a bonafide test, it does offer an opportunity to note the flaws in individual play. To make such testing more efficient, it would be well to have more than one judge score a player. In the following chart, used to check players in action, the scorers place dots in the appropriate column.

RECORD OF PLAYER IN ACTION

Name: _____

Position: _____

	The Pass						The Set up						Penalties				Assists
	From Easy Ball			Diffi-cult Ball			From Easy Ball			Diffi-cult Ball			Touching Net	Over the Net	Over Line	Out of Position	
	Good	Fair	Poor	Good	Fair	Poor	Good	Fair	Poor	Good	Fair	Poor					
Points	5	3	0	10	5	1	5	3	0	10	5	1					
First game																	
Second game																	
Total																	
Remarks:																	

THE BRADY TEST. George F. Brady of the University of Tennessee published in the March, 1945, edition of the *Research Quarterly* a paper on "Volleyball Playing Ability," in which he discussed the problem of measuring the volleyball playing ability of college men. The test used in this project was easy to administer and was found to be quite practical during the years that the author was in charge of the volleyball program at Springfield College. This included regular classes and varsity experience.

The test is conducted on the following basis: A goal area is marked on the wall, with a base line 11 feet 6 inches from the floor and 5 feet in width. The side lines extend upward from the base to the ceiling. The player stands in front of the goal area with the ball. At the signal to go, he tosses the ball against the wall and hits it on the rebound.

To score, the ball must hit the wall on or between the boundary lines. Each time it hits in the goal, a point is scored. If the ball gets out of control, it is started again as at the beginning of the test. The player is timed for 1 minute. Only the successful legal volleys that hit within the goal are recorded as the score. Thrown balls or one-handed passes do not count. Scores ranged from 20 to 50. There is favorable correlation in the Brady scores and general ability to play the game.

Passing Test for Beginners. Stretch a heavy string across one court, 10 feet in height and 15 feet back from the net. Divide the front of this court into three sections, each 10 by 15 feet. Each of these sections will have the following value in points: right forward, 10 points; center forward, 20 points; left forward, 5 points.

Player A, the testee, will stand in the right back area of the court. The testor, B, stands in the center of the court near the net, facing A. B tosses the ball over the string to A, who tries to pass the ball back over the string to the center-forward area. Points are scored according to where the ball hits the floor, providing it first goes over the string. Ten trials should be taken.

Passing Test for Advanced Players. Use same set up as test before. However, in this test, B moves to the center of the opposite court and serves the ball to A, who will stand in the center-back area of the court. Score the same as the first test.

Distance Passing Test. Player B stands near the center of the net, facing the rear of the court. Player A stands back of the end line near the center. B tosses the ball to A, who hits it with sufficient force to travel over the net. Count points in relation to where the ball lands in the court:

Failure to clear the net.................................. 0 points
Ball clears net, lands within 10 feet of net............... 5 points
Ball clears net, lands between 10 and 20 feet of net.........10 points
Ball clears net, lands 20 to 30 feet from net................15 points

Handling-the-Ball Test (see Diagram 13). This test requires a 12-foot step-ladder or staging from which the ball can be dropped. This is placed on the side line, 8 feet from the end line of the court. A string is placed across the court at a 10-foot height. It is parallel to the net and 10 feet from it. The front half of the court is divided into three sections of 10 by 15 feet with the following values: right forward area, 10 points; center forward area, 5 points; left center area, 2 points.

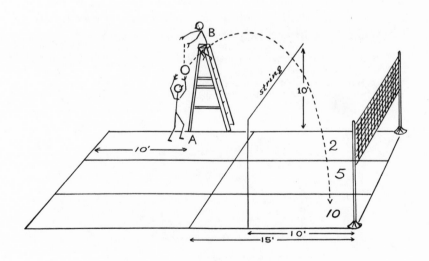

Diag. 13. Test for handling of the ball.

Player B drops the ball to A, who passes it over the string into one of the three sections. If the ball goes under the string, into the net, or out of bounds, no points are scored. With the ball being played from the left side of the court, the right-forward area has the greatest value. Ten trials should be taken. The scorer should record errors in play, such as low passes, ball out of bounds, or hitting the net.

Precision Passing. A basketball goal may be used for precision passing. The testor, B, stands under the goal and tosses the ball to A, who stands 5 feet in front of the goal. A attempts to pass the ball into the goal. Points counted are:

> Ball goes through goal without touching rim ....10 points
> Ball hits the rim and goes into goal .... 5 points
> Ball hits rim but does not go in.......................... 2 points
> Ball hits the backboard .... 0 points

Volleyball Goal Test. This test requires a volleyball goal made of bamboo, held together by wire and adhesive tape (see Diagram 14). This goal has the following dimensions: 5 feet long, 2½ feet wide. The back uprights are 3 feet in length. The supporting rods are joined to make a fairly substantial frame. By adding a couple of hooks on the top back rod, the frame can be hung or fastened to a basketball goal, the bottom cross rod resting on the goal support.

The test should be scored as follows:

> Passed into goal without touching rim or backboard ....10 points
> Ball hitting rim of goal and falling into goal .... 5 points
> Ball hitting rim and not going in .... 2 points
> Ball hitting backboard or under goal .... 0 points

Passing Test. Toss the ball to the testee, A, standing in the rear of the court. A passes the ball to set-up, B, in the center-forward area. Score points in relation to the accuracy of the pass:

> B does not have to move to get the ball .... 5 points
> B has to take more than one step .... 3 points
> B has to take more than three steps .... 1 point
> If pass goes out of bounds or into net .... 0 point

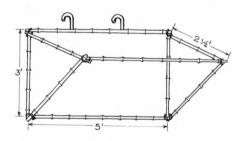

Diag. 14. Volleyball goal.

4

Serving the Ball

The first play in the game of volleyball is the serve. The rules specify that the server shall hit the ball over the net into the opponents' court with his hand, fist, or arm while standing in the service area in back of the end line. Teachers should point out that the service is an offensive play and that only the serving team has the opportunity to score. Therefore, learning how to serve the ball safely into the opponents' court is an important objective. As players increase in skills and general playing ability, the nature of the service changes from a safe serve to one that becomes a potent offensive weapon, in which hard-driven, tricky balls tend to delude the receivers. Many of these serves are extremely difficult to handle, and some of them rocket across the net to score a point.

In view of the rotation feature of the game, each player takes his turn at serving. This means that every player must be able to serve the ball efficiently and effectively. The novice should first master the underhand method of serving and should place the ball consistently in the most difficult spots for the opponents to return.

In addition to the development of the more difficult serves, the screen has come into modern play as an aid to the server and the beginning stages of the flight of the ball. The effectiveness of the serve is increased, as opponents have less time to play the ball.

Rules permit players (except the server) to move into any place on the court as long as they retain their rotation order. They are free to move their hands to the side or over their own heads in an attempt to further hide the server and the serve. The server crouches low behind the screen and directs his serve to weaker players or attempts a low serve that just clears the net.

A careful program of conditioning and practice drills, coupled with testing and practice games, will do much to develop serving skills. At this point it is well to review the general serving rules:

1. In serving the ball, a player must stand in back of the end line of the court. He may step forward onto the line and into the court after the ball has been contacted.

31

2. The ball may be hit with the hand, fist, or arm.
3. The ball must go over the net without touching it and land either on or inside the boundary lines.
4. The ball must not touch any object or fixture of the net before it lands in the opponents' court.

THE UNDERHAND SERVE

The underhand method is the surest way to serve the ball into the opponents' court. This method of serving is easy to learn, and beginners quickly pick up the fundamental techniques.

In teaching the fundamentals of the serve, the writer has had favorable experience in teaching these skills with students lined up about 20 feet in front of a wall. It is much easier to center attention on the techniques of the serve in this position. When these have been explained, demonstrated, and practiced, the move to the court is much easier. This formation also speeds up the teaching process and offers a splendid opportunity to observe weaknesses.

TECHNIQUE OF UNDERHAND SERVE. Take a position facing the wall, with a comfortable stance, left foot advanced (see Diagram 15). Hold the ball in the palm of the left hand. Place the left hand in front of the right thigh, fingers pointing to the right and the thumb pointing forward. The weight is on the forward foot, and the left knee is slightly bent while the right is straight. Swing the serving arm (right) directly backward in a smooth pendulum-like movement. At the same time shift the weight of the body to the right foot and bend the right knee as the body twists to the right. The left hand, which holds the ball, also moves slightly backward with the sway of the body and swing of the arm.

Diag. 15. The underhand serve.

At this point, the serving hand is held in an open, clawlike position. The right arm swings forward in a pendulum-like movement as the body weight shifts to the left foot, forcing the body to twist to the left. In this movement, power is added to the serve by straightening the legs, then twisting the hips to the left, and slightly arching the back. The ball is not tossed but held in the palm of the left hand and hit with the open right hand at the end of the forward swing. After the ball is hit, the right foot comes forward in a natural follow-through. Caution should be taken to avoid any throwing movement in the final action; eyes should be kept on the ball at all times. After hitting the ball with the open hand, continue the follow-through upward, the serving hand finishing high in front of the head. This follow-through aids the server in getting under the ball and hitting it forward and upward.

Practice the serving movement without the ball, having the students sway or rock backward and forward in time with the serving arm. Be sure to emphasize the importance of the shifting of the body weight and the necessity of getting under the ball. Also call attention to the fact that the arm stroke should be in the anterior-posterior plane (this is directly forward and back). Some beginners have a tendency to hit the ball in a side swinging action. This makes control difficult. Have the students practice serving the ball against the wall, and watch for weaknesses.

Faults generally made by novices include:

1. Tossing the ball rather than hitting it off the holding hand.
2. Swinging the serving arm in a sideward movement.
3. Lifting the head and taking the eyes off the ball just as it is being struck.
4. Holding the ball too far forward, thereby losing power to get it over the net.
5. Incomplete follow-through of serving arm, ending swing below level of shoulders.
6. Tendency to use the closed fist for serve. This is not good practice for a beginner. Control is lacking.
7. Striking too low on the ball and sending it too high.

As stated before, skilled teams utilize the serve as a highly effective weapon and consider it a forceful factor in offensive play, a point which should be stressed with beginners.

Other possibilities of using the underhand serve include the heel-of-hand serve.

HEEL-OF-HAND SERVE. Up to this point it has been suggested that the serve be made by hitting the ball with the open hand held in a clawlike position. Fingers are kept close together and the ball is hit with the palmar surface and heel of the hand. As soon as the underhand serve has been mastered

Diag. 16. Heel-of-the-hand serve.

with the open hand, it is well to introduce the heel-of-hand serve. The preliminary action is the same as described for the open underhand serve, the only difference being in the use of the heel of the hand instead of the palms and fingers. The hand is still open, but the fingers are dropped downward and the heel of the hand is raised. The ball is hit with the heel of the hand, just below the dead center of the ball, making for a curved flight and causing the ball to jump or slide. If the ball has little or no spin, it tends to float. Students should be cautioned not to hit the ball with too much force. They should work for control, as this is one of the most effective services in today's volleyball (see Diagram 16).

THE OUT. The stance is the same as previously described. The ball is held in front of the body in the left hand, with the valve to the right. Swing the right arm backward and then forward with a driving motion. The arm and hand come forward with the thumb leading and the fingers pointing downward. Hit the right side of the ball with the palm and fingers in a twisting movement made possible by rotating the arm and thumb inward toward the body. If the ball is hit with sufficient force, the path of the ball will follow a baseball "out-curve," moving from right to left. This serve is effective when it is placed between two opponents. It serves as a change of pace and is a comparatively safe serve to use.

THE IN. The action of this serve is opposite to that of the out-curve in respect to movement of the serving hand and arm. Hold the ball with the valve facing to the left. The preliminary arm movement is the same as for the underhand serve, but as the hand nears the ball on the forward swing, it is rotated outward to the right, and the ball is hit on its left side with the palm of the right hand, with the little finger leading the action. The forward swing of the arm and the forceful rotation of the hand impart enough force to send the ball over the net, curving from left to right. This is a difficult serve to execute and calls for much skill and control. The server's arm should be thoroughly warmed up before attempting this serve.

THE DROP. The ball is held in the left hand, palm up with the valve down, in front of the right shoulder. The right arm swings backward in the

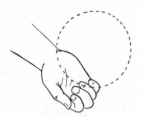

Diag. 17. The knuckle ball—the floater.

shoulder-height horizontal plane, with the palm turned upward. It swings forward in the same relative position. The action is similar to the forward pass movement of a football player. The ball is hit from underneath with a slicing or cutting action which imparts a reverse spin on the ball. This sends the ball forward into the air, in an ascending arc. As it reaches the back of the opponents' court, the "english" on the ball, meeting with air resistance, makes it drop. Many times the ball will land "in court" when it looks as though it were going out of the court.

THE KNUCKLE BALL—THE FLOATER. The ball is held in the left hand and the swing of the right arm is as for the underhand serve. The ball is struck with the heel of the hand and the first knuckles of the fingers which are flexed, exposing the fingernails. The thumb is parallel to the hand and index finger (see Diagram 17). On the forward swing of the serving arm, the ball is hit at the dead center of the back of the ball. At the moment of contact, the hand is abruptly withdrawn from the ball. Players should avoid the use of too much force because it reduces control and also the "floating" qualities. This is a popular serve in modern volleyball.

THE FIST SERVE. The closed fist may be used in three positions for serving. First with the palm turned upward. The fingers are flexed, the thumb rests against the closed fingers, and the ball is hit with the fingers and heel of the upturned fist. The second fist serve is the back-hand serve, using the back of the hand as the hitting surface. The third method is the index finger and thumb serve. The ball is hit with the thumb extended and the first finger flexed, with the arm rotated inward so as to place this hitting surface as the leading part in the movement. The fist ball is difficult to control, and if used, it would be well to caution players against hitting the ball too forcefully.

THE OVERHAND SERVE

Much experimentation is taking place as to how the ball should be hit; some cup the fingers, some use the fist in various positions, many use the heel of the hand, and some combine this with the knuckles. Some even take a running start to hit the ball, and others jump into the air. Many are experimenting with a nonspin type of serve, with the valve placed in different positions. All these suggestions and many more, along with the screen, make the game a more difficult one for the receiver of the serve.

After learning the fundamentals of the underhand serve, a beginner is ready to learn the skills of the overhand serve. It is a standard method of serving in modern volleyball, and hence a discussion of the various overhand serves follows.

THE FUNDAMENTAL OVERHAND SERVE. The correct stance for each player will vary, but a novice should be advised to stand several inches in back of the service line, facing the net rather than the side of the court. The right-handed server is balanced on both feet, and his left foot is firmly set and pointed toward the net. The right foot is placed backward at a comfortable distance, and the heel is on a line with the left foot, which points on an angle to the right. This position forms a good base for action.

Hold the ball in front of the right hip with both hands. The arms are flexed in a comfortable position. The movement starts with a slight knee bend and extension as the ball is tossed to a position just above the head and in front of the right shoulder. As the toss is being made, the weight is shifted backward to the right foot. Following this, the serving arm moves upward and backward, with the elbow leading, bringing the upper arm into a horizontal position. At the same time the back is arched and the body twists to the right. As the ball drops to the desired height, the right elbow leads in the start of the whipping action of the serve by moving forward. From this point on, the arm action is similar to a baseball catcher's peg. The forearm,

Diag. 18. The overhand serve.

wrists, and fingers travel forward and downward in a snapping, forceful manner. The ball is hit above the head with a cupped hand so that the heel, palm, and fingers get into play (see Diagram 18).

When contact is made with the ball, the following action takes place. The right leg straightens, shifting the weight to the left leg and swinging the right hip forward, following through the whipping action. The forearm continues the power generated by the upper arm in a forward-downward drive. The wrist snaps forward at the last instant like the final action of the shot putter.

If a server puts a great deal of body weight into his serve, he should take care not to step into the court before he contacts the ball. However, he should move quickly into a defensive position immediately after serving the ball.

Serving the ball may be a highly coordinated movement in which many parts of the body are used. Teachers should be on the alert for the following weaknesses, which many beginners show:

1. A tendency to throw the ball too high, making it more difficult to hit.
2. A tendency to throw the ball too far forward, making for a low serve.
3. A tendency to throw the ball too far to one side.
4. A tendency to twist the body, sending the ball to the side.
5. Using a straight arm action rather than the bent arm action.
6. Using the fist.

The serves discussed subsequently are advanced techniques. Individual differences must be considered in adapting any of the suggestions made.

THE FLOATER (Overhand No Spin Serve). The flight of this service may be unpredictable, wavering, tricky, and swerving; hence its favored use in the game. It is in all probability the hardest ball for the defense to handle. The ball is usually served low, just skimming the net. It forces even skilled players to make hasty moves, thereby making the reception of the service an uncertainty rather than a sure thing. It makes the recovery play a defensive move rather than an offensive one. This is an easy and effective serve to learn, and it is not difficult to control, once the fundamentals are mastered. Too much speed reduces the control and also the floating qualities.

The ball should not be thrown too high, a low toss being much more efficient. The arm and body action are identical to the movements in the foregoing overhand serve; the difference is in how the ball is hit. However, in tossing the ball up for the serve, the valve should be facing forward.

The ball should be struck with the heel of the hand and the first knuckles of the fingers so as to hit the ball in the dead center or just above with a slight upward movement. The ball should be hit so that there is no spin on it and it will be in a dead float to the net. As it passes over the net, the valve causes the ball to spin in one direction or another with the resulting sliding, jumping, and floating characteristics.

Other methods of hitting the ball include the use of the heel of the hand and the fist. In these serves, the snapping action of the wrist should be emphasized when contact with the ball has been made. The follow-through is limited.

CURVING SERVES. The "in" and "out" curves as previously described in the underhand service may be executed in an overhand manner.

THE DROP. The technique of this serve is difficult to learn, since it calls for a highly coordinated movement. The ball is tossed above the head as for the regular overhand serve. The ball should be hit in such a manner that the finger tips make first contact on the upper half of the back of the ball. The heel of the hand follows in quick succession with a forceful impact that starts the ball forward in a clockwise or forward spin on it. The body action is a backward bend using the regular stance, followed by a whipping action of the arm. The body straightens and twists to the left, adding power to the serve. The forward spin of the ball tends to make the ball slide off the hands of the receiver. Another advantage of this serve is to have the ball "drop" into the court when it seems to be headed out of bounds.

THE SIDE BEND (Hook Serve). A right-handed server stands with his left side to the net, feet astride in a comfortable stance. The ball is tossed slightly above the head. The body bends sideward to the right, with the right arm dropping downward. As the right arm, slightly bent, starts its upward and forward swing, the body bends to the left, and the serving arm continues on to hit the ball. The hitting hand is in a clawlike position and imparts a forward spin to the ball much in the same manner as the "drop" described above. Tremendous power may be exerted in this serve by the coordination

Diag. 19.   The side-bend serve.

of the swing accompanied by a forceful side body bending movement. This is a very satisfactory method of serving but requires considerable practice and patience to acquire the necessary skill to control it (see Diagram 19).

STATUE OF LIBERTY SERVE. Some players eliminate tossing the ball into the air by holding it in the air with the left hand similar to a golf tee. The ball is held high above the right shoulder. The right arm swings backward and then forward to hit the ball off the hand. With this serve, a player has excellent control over the ball.

THE SIDE SWING SERVE. The server faces the net in a comfortable stance or stands with his side to the net. The ball is tossed up to the right side of the server as the right arm swings backward in a slightly flexed position in a near horizontal plane. The forward action of the arm is a sweeping movement as the body turns to the left, and the ball is hit with the open hand, fist, or heel of the hand. The arm continues to follow through as the server steps into the court. This serve may be effective with taller players; however, it calls for exceptional control.

THE BODY TWISTER SERVE. The server stands with his back to the net. He tosses the ball over his head and hits it with a forceful swing brought about by twisting the body a half-turn to the left. The right arm swings up and forward to the left to hit the ball in such a manner that tremendous overspin is imparted to it. Occasionally, a player will develop an effective serve with this method.

The key to successful serving is persistency in learning to control the ball.

PLACEMENT OF THE SERVE

The primary objective of this section on placement is to introduce the beginner to certain fundamentals of play. Later we shall consider advanced techniques and formations that are in keeping with modern volleyball. The beginner should recognize that there are certain positions on the floor which are more difficult for the opponents to play. With this in mind, prior to the serve, the beginner should glance at the formation of the receiving team and make up his mind as to the best place to serve the ball. It is assumed that for novice play, the 3–3 system is being used. There will be three set-up players and three spikers.

In Diagram 2 (page 12) note that opponents have their spikers in the left and right positions with the set-up playing the center-forward position. The first choice would be to serve the ball to the right-back position (the far corner of the court). The recovery of this serve calls for a long pass to the set-up, who is forced to turn away from his attack in recovering the ball for the set up. If the ball is served to the center of the court, the center-back player is in a good position to make an easy pass to the set-up. With the opponents in the same position, a second choice would be to serve the ball into the left-back corner of the court, again forcing a long pass on the recovery.

It will be noted in Diagram 3 (Page 12) that the teams have rotated and the opposing team is in a different formation, with the spiker playing in the center position and his set-up in the right-forward position. The first choice would be to serve the ball to the left-back player, who is obliged to make a long pass to the right forward set-up. If the ball is served into the right-back position, it is a second choice, since the pass may be made directly forward to the set-up, who is in a relatively favorable position.

In general a ball served to the far corners is always a better placement than to any point in the center of the court. Sometimes it is possible to drop the ball over the net into the opponents' court near the side lines. When the screen is used, the ball may clear the screen and net and drop into the center of the court. The strength of this play is in its deceptiveness as it shoots across the net after being hidden by the screen. Serves should be made so that opponents have to move to get the ball. Look for open spots on the court and direct the serve to such open spaces. Work to keep the opposition guessing where the ball is to come. Place the ball between two players, especially if you have been successful in confusing them in previous serves. If the screen is used, be sure to develop a system of team play in which the screen is working in the right direction.

GENERAL CONSIDERATIONS

POINT OF SERVICE. The rules permit a person to serve from any point in back of the 30-foot end line. The safest position to take in serving the ball is within the center 10 feet of the serving area. In this position a player has a greater chance of keeping his serves in the court. As skills improve, the server may move to the right or left in keeping with the particular kind of a serve he desires to use.

Before serving, the player should take a quick glance to see that his team mates are in their correct positions. He should be ready to call for a change in the position of the screen or to correct overlapping, etc. In addition he should spot the position of the opponents and occasionally should call for a rearrangement in the subsequent plays.

A server should not be hurried. He should concentrate on making the best possible serve, and he is given a reasonable amount of time for this.

PRELIMINARY WARM-UPS. Players should participate in a preliminary series of warm-up exercises. Going in to a game "cold" is poor practice. Special attention should be given to the conditioning of fingers and hands. Reception of hard serves is the cause of many extremity injuries, and these are detrimental to efficient play.

PRACTICE SUGGESTIONS

Practice 1.   Divide the group into three sections, placing three players in file formation on each side of the net, facing each other.   The head player in each file stands about 20 feet back from the net.   The three files on one side face three opposite files.   Three balls are used.   The drill starts with the lead player serving the ball to the head of the opposite file, who catches it and then returns the serve, after which he moves to the rear of his file.   Increase the distance from the net until the serve is made from the regular serving area.

Practice 2.   The underhand serve is the subject for practice here.   Players take position in back of serving line and practice serving the ball, using various methods such as heel of the hand, knuckles, and fist.

Practice 3.   Using the overhand serve, hitting the ball with the open hand, the heel of the hand, the knuckle-floater ball, the "in" and the "out" are subjects for practice.

Practice 4.   Place a bushel basket in the center of the right-back area and see how many players are able to hit the basket.   Change target to the left-back area.

Practice 5.   Have one team line up ready to receive the service.   Have the server serve the ball between players.

Practice 6.   Place three men across the court about 20 feet back from the net.   Serve the ball to these back-field players and have them concentrate in getting a good pass forward to the center of the court.   Record the number of serves that are difficult to handle.

Practice 7.   Have players serve the ball from different positions along the serving line at 2-foot intervals, starting at one of the corners.   Record the number of successful serves made to the right-back and left-back areas.

Practice 8.   Have each player practice throwing the ball to different heights in order to learn the height that is most favorable for his particular style of serving.   When this has been determined, hang a target at the correct height.   A string may be stretched across the court, or targets may be hung from a suspended wire.

Practice 9.   The best practice drill is to have two players on opposite sides of the court serving back and forth to each other.   This means that the ball is being observed at all times and reduces the danger of players being hit. Players should concentrate on control, power, and placement.   Careless and aimless attempts to serve the ball in unorthodox ways should not be tolerated. The practice of getting every ball into the court should be the goal of all players.

TESTS

Testing is time consuming but rewarding, especially if the tests motivate players to improve their skills.

GENERAL TEST.   The most valid test for serving is to grade a player while the game is in progress.   In such a study, it is well to have more than one testor.   Retests should be made at intervals to note improvement.   The main criteria to consider in building such a test would include:

1. Where the ball lands (in or out of court or into net).
2. Placement to corners, or to the center of court.
3. Nature of serve, speed, curve, lob.
4. Nature of recovery, easy or difficult.
5. Was it an "ace"?

The accompanying chart is suggested for studying a player's serve. Dots indicating the results of the serve are placed in the appropriate column.

SERVING RECORD											
Date: _____					Name: _____						
	Hits Net	Foot Fault	Out End	Out Left	Out Right	Lob Serve	Over Speed	Over Curve	Placed Corner	Ace	Final Score
Scoring values	0	0	0	0	0	1	4	4	5	10	
First game											
Second game											
Third game											
Comments											

RECOVERY TEST.   Another form of testing would be to record the nature of the recovery of the serve by the receiving player.   If the serve is:

Received and passed with ease............................ 0 points
Difficult to handle, resulting in a fair setup .... 5 points
Difficult to handle, resulting in a poor setup .... 7 points
"Ace-ing" the ball..10 points

PLACEMENT TESTS

Test 1.   Divide the court into six sections 10 by 15 feet (see Diagram 20). Score as follows if the serve lands:

In the left-back area ....10 points
In right-back area .... 8 points
In left-front area .... 5 points
In right-front area .... 3 points
In center-back area .... 2 points
In center-forward area .... 1 point

3	8
1	2
5	10

NET

Diag. 20.   Court sections.

The server should attempt to place the ball in the left-back area, which has the highest scoring value.   If a ball touches a line, it is scored as a hit.

Test 2.   Repeat Test 1, using the overhand serve.

Test 3.   Divide the court in halves with a line running parallel to the side lines.   Using the underhand method of serving, hit five serves into the right half of the court and five into the left half.   Count ten points for each successful serve.

Test 4.   With the same set up as Test 3, serve the ball, using the overhand method.

Test 5.   Divide the court into four sections, the two front sections of the court to measure 15 by 20 feet; the two back, 15 by 10 feet.   Serve the ball, using the overhand method of serving, and score as follows if the ball lands in:

Left-rear section	20 points
Right-rear section	15 points
Left-front section	10 points
Right-front section	5 points

Test 6. Curve Test.   The object of this test is to serve the ball into the opposite court so that it will curve, float, or drop.   Count the number of times out of ten successful serves that the ball curves.   Use the underhand method first and then the overhand.

Test 7.   Newspapers may be used as a target for spot serving.   Six double sheets make a good-sized target for testing.   Wooden frames, 6 by 6 feet, may also be made for such a test.   Additional frames of greater size may be used to advantage.   With the 6 by 6 foot target, count score as follows:

For each hit	5 points
Within 3 feet of target	2 points
Within 6 feet of target	1 point

5

The Attack

The "attack," "spike," or "kill" is regarded as the most spectacular and colorful part of the game. It is a dynamic maneuver, in which a player must jump into the air, hit a moving target with such force and direction that it will pass over an 8-foot net, and evade the opposition who not only form a blocking barrier at the net but are skilled in recovering terrific drives. In team play, the attack is usually made on the third play of the ball. However, it should be noted that an attack may also be made on either the first or second play, depending on the position of the ball and the readiness and ability of the spiker. In view of the increased number of blockers now allowed, there is no doubt that spiking skill calls for the finest coordination to be found in any of our modern games.

Like other skills, spiking can be taught. The following information is geared for the beginner. The ability to jump, body balance, quick thinking, and explosive arm power make up the ingredients of successful spiking.

FUNDAMENTALS OF THE ATTACK

Players who aspire to play an attack position must have considerable power in their legs. They must have stamina for periods of continuous jumping, and they must have the ability to make a smashing drive while suspended in the air. The coordination of these movements into a smooth effective play is an attainment of high order. In addition, a spiker must be able to sense the positions of his opponents in the block at the net and the remaining defense on the floor. Further, he must be able to retrieve blocks that are returned, by quickly shifting from an offensive play to a defensive one. Since the set-up passer is the key to successful spiking, the set-up player and the spiker must work together as a unit. Without a good set, the attack player loses effectiveness.

PHYSICAL CONDITIONING. Proper conditioning of the legs is the first step in attack performance. It is recommended that lesson plans include a general conditioning work-out for players. This will ensure a proper warming-up period and will also improve body tone. At least 15 minutes should be taken for this preliminary program, especially at the beginning of the season. On the premise that "function makes structure," the following exercises will be helpful:

Exercise 1. Running. In place on the toes, or on an indoor track, or out of doors.

Exercise 2. Knee Bending. Full knee bends, with or without weights. Weights have been found to aid greatly in building leg strength. Rest weights on shoulders if a barbell is available.

Exercise 3. Jumping. In place, facing the net, see how far above the net you can reach. Jump off both feet or make continuous short jumps off both feet. Hop on one foot in place, then the other.

Exercise 4. Skipping. Start with short skips; then lengthen to extended skipping.

Exercise 5. Rope Skipping.

Exercise 6. Sargent Jump. For complete details, see page 53. This test will give an indication of leg power. Student faces wall and reaches above head, marking with chalk his highest reach. He then turns with side to wall and springs into air, marking the maximum height of his jump. His score will be the difference between the two marks.

FUNDAMENTAL MOVEMENTS. In view of the difficulty of this maneuver, it will be introduced in several steps.

Hitting the Ball (standing). The first objective in learning how to spike a ball is how to hit it. In athletic activities it has been demonstrated that greater power is released when the striking arm is in the bent-arm position. It should be noted that players who use the straight-arm action in hitting the ball have a tendency to throw the ball rather than to hit it. This should be avoided, as it is a violation of the rules. A second principle in the attack is that the ball should be hit on top rather than on the sides or bottom. The drive should be downward. Balls that are hit on the lower half will be directed upward and will tend to go out of the court.

The following exercise may be included as a part of the drill work in the warm-up conditioning period. The instructor explains and demonstrates the whipping action of the arm, wrist, and hand, along with body coordination. This furnishes an opportunity to explain the fundamental movements of the attack. It quickly captures the interest and attention of beginners. Following this demonstration, the teacher will lead his class through the hitting action without the ball. This provides a good exercise and at the same time gives novices an opportunity to feel the movement. Following the exercise, divide the class into groups of five or six players each.

Diag. 21. Hitting the ball off the hand.

The next exercise is a preliminary in learning how to spike. Each player, in turn, practices hitting the ball to the floor. Pupils should be cautioned to keep their eyes on the ball, for it is possible for the ball to bound back and hit the spiker in the face.

Hold the ball in the left hand, palm up in front of the waist (see Diagram 21). Take a firm stance, with the weight on the balls of the feet and body erect. The movement starts with a forward lean of the body as the right arm is lifted to the right side in a bent-arm position, the elbow leading the action. The elbow continues upward to head height with the hand following. At this point, the elbow changes to a downward direction, forcing the forearm into a perpendicular position. This position is maintained for a split second as the forearm starts a snapping action forward and downward, like the crack of a whip. The upper arm rotates on the shoulder joint. As the arm comes down and as the hand hits the ball to the floor, there is a flexing, whipping, slapping movement of the wrist and hand. The ball may be hit with the heel of the hand, but in this drill, teachers advise the use of the cupped palm of the open hand. If the movement is executed properly, great power will be released through the final whip of the wrist and hand. The action of this movement is again similar to the peg of the baseball catcher who whips the ball to second base.

To get more power into the hit, have the student step forward with the right leg and twist the body to the left as the weight is transferred to the right leg. This action approximates a falling movement. Players should be cautioned not to toss the ball into the air prior to hitting it. There is a general tendency to do this.

With these combined efforts, the ball may be driven to the floor with such force that it will bound high into the air. There is a sense of elation in hitting the ball in this manner. It gives players an opportunity to "feel" the power and thrill of spiking the ball. Have players practice this movement until they have mastered it. Be sure that the elbow leads both in the action upward and in the first downward movement. Be on the alert to discover and correct players who use a straight-arm attack.

Hitting the Ball in the Air.   Hold the ball in both hands about waist high in front of the body.   Jump into the air.   It will be difficult to avoid tossing the ball.   However, it can be done and will make the ball a much easier target to hit.   At the height of the jump, release the ball and attempt to hit it while you are suspended in the air.   The correct position for the ball when contacted is approximately chest height.   The object of this position is to have the ball so placed that the spiker will be able to hit on top of the ball.   From this point on, the arm action is the same as explained above.   The body comes in for greater play as the spiking arm leads the body in a twisting movement to the left.   Players should land on both feet.

Hitting a Moving Ball.   In the first two drills the ball has been under the control of the player.   From this point on, the beginner will face actual game situations in which the ball will come to him for the attack.   Timing is an all-important factor in this action.   Toss the ball into the air in front of a player who will jump and attempt to hit the ball with the fundamental whip-arm action.   Keep the ball at a comparatively low height, 7 or 8 feet, in order to reduce the degree of difficulty which the beginning spiker faces.   There is a tendency for the novice to reach up with a straight arm and hit the ball, especially if the ball is placed in back, forcing a player to reach for it.   Stress the principle that the best attack is made when the spiker is able to come down on the ball and not have to reach backward for it.

Diag. 22.   Basic action of the attack.

Jump Attack from Standing Position (Diagram 22).   Lower the net to 7 feet (or lower) for these practice drills.   The player stands with his left side close to the net, facing the teacher who will toss the ball into the air for the attack. The lowered net will reduce the degree of difficulty and enable the student to practice the whip-arm action, which is so important.   Coach the students to smash the ball as they did when they practiced hitting the ball off their hands in the first drill.

Toss the ball about 10 feet or more into the air above the net so that it will descend in front of the attack player.   As the ball approaches, the attack will prepare to spring into the air.   His stance may be compared to that of a broad jumper who swings both arms backward, bends his knees, and flexes his body at the waist.   The weight is carried on the toes, ready for the upward swing.   As the attack leaves the floor, the right arm is raised so that the elbow is slightly above the shoulder and to the side, while the forearm is raised in the anterior-posterior plane to about a 45-degree angle, the wrist drawn back, and the hand cupped and facing forward.   As the ball passes through the attacking area, the body comes forward and twists to the left, the right shoulder is drawn in and down toward the body, the forearm moves downward, and at the same instant the wrist adds the finishing touch to the stroke as it snaps forward and downward on the upper half of the ball.   In the spring, the body turns toward the net.

When the ball is hit, the body executes a sharp twist to the left, which brings the attack directly facing the net.   This turn is assisted by the sweep of the upper arm and the snapping action of the forearm and the wrist.   The arm continues its swing in front of and across the chest and not in a forward thrust, which could make for a foul in touching the net.   After the ball has been hit, the player returns to the floor facing the net.   The twist of the body, the dropping of the shoulders, and the final snap of the wrist are fundamental in giving power to the spike.

Players should be encouraged to practice the attack skills and to develop a whiplike action in hitting the ball.   They should soon learn that it will be necessary to learn how to place the ball, i.e., to drive it down rather than straight ahead, and to cut and slice against opponents who use the block in their defensive play.

The Running Attack.   For the great majority of players, and especially for the beginner, it is not necessary for the attack to plan for a long run in spiking the ball.   The spiker must have control of body weight while jumping, and he should not fall or step forward when the attack is completed.   Spiking requires a vertical take-off.   Having too great a run will tend to force the attack into the net.   The teacher will note that this is a fault of many beginners.

There is a great variety of take-offs for the attack.   One player will run along the net and jump. Another will come in on an angle; some will jump and spike from a stand, and some will come straight in. Some will use the take-off from one foot and some will use both feet. However, the most popular spike approach in volleyball today is the straight-in or slight angle two-leg take-off. This method is described in detail, as it is especially applicable for beginners (see Diagram 23).

The spiker stands about 8 feet from the net, being prepared to make a straight-ahead approach or to come in on a slight angle. The feet are on a line as the movement starts. Advance the left foot about 2 feet 6 inches, a comfortable step. The arms remain at the side. A forward step is taken by the right foot (measuring approximately 3 feet 10 inches), and the left arm swings forward and the right back. The left foot now steps forward about 3 feet 6 inches. As the player prepares for the jump, both arms are swung backward, and the right foot scoots forward beside the left foot. As this last step is taken, both knees are bent in a crouch position, the body is tilted forward and flexed at the waist. Both arms are flexed; the left to the left side of the body and the right swung backward in the flexed position preliminary to a sweeping upward swing when the jump is made. The feet are close together for the take-off stance (6 to 8 inches apart). In fact the action of the attack jump is similar to that of the standing broad jumper as he gathers force in preparing for the jump. A preliminary fundamental is to be sure that the forward-moving force is changed to an upward, vertical one.

With the spring into the air, the attack is ready for the spike. The right arm swings upward in a bent arm position with the elbow leading. The legs and body straighten, and the ball is hit with a downward, sweeping, snapping cut on the ball. The beginner will have to take particular care to stay out of the net, as the tendency is to follow through into the net when he hits the ball. To avoid this, he should continue the spiking action of the right arm across his body. A slight turn to the left will also help. On returning to the

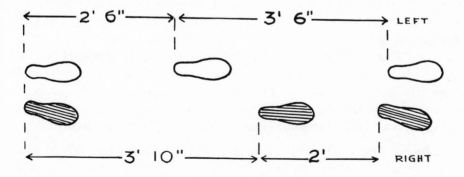

Diag. 23. Attack foot action.

floor, players should be coached to land on two feet and to be on the alert for the next play.

VARIATIONS OF THE ATTACK. There are many variations of the attack which a spiker will have to consider. However, it will be well for the beginner to master the art of timing and hitting the ball, using as a guide the fundamental techniques that have been presented in this chapter.

The methods of attack described subsequently are advanced plays and should not be used by players until they have mastered the fundamentals of the attack.

The Low Set up Power Attack. For this attack, the ball is set up 1 or 2 feet above and close to the net. In extremely low sets, the attack leaves the floor at the same instant the ball is set up. It is recognized that close teamwork and exceptional timing are necessary in this play. In this attack, the spiker may hit the ball at three distinct points: first, while it is on its way up; second, at the height of the pass; and third, when it is descending.

The low set ball travels slowly and pauses for an instant prior to descending, giving the spiker an unusual opportunity to hit it. The low set up can be faked as a high set up toward one side of the court, but at the last moment the set up is made backward over the set-up's head to the opposite side of the court. The low set does not give the opposition much time to set for the block. Coaches will do well to spend time in training the spikers to use this attack.

Straight-Arm Attack (Windmill). Some players use the straight-arm attack most effectively. Beginners find this a comparatively easy method to use, but as has been emphasized, it is inadvisable for them to use·in view of the tendency to throw the ball. The attack brings into play the bent elbow on the upward swing of the arm. At the top of the swing, the arm is straightened and snaps down with power on the ball. After contact with the ball, the elbow should be flexed to increase both the force of the hit and the downward angle of the ball. The same flexion prevents following through and fouling at the net. The continuous arm-swinging action prevents one from throwing the ball.

In the "windmill" attack, the arm is used in the fully extended position when the ball is hit. The right arm begins the attack in front of the body and swiftly describes a counterclockwise circle. It completes the action in front of the face when the arm, wrist, and hand snap down vigorously on the ball. This is a highly skilled movement that calls for exceptional timing.

The Double Attack. It is at this point that the ambidextrous player gains the spotlight. The ability to jump into the air and hit the ball with either hand is a rare accomplishment and an asset to offensive play. With the speedy development of the game, this tactic should receive greater consideration. Both arms are raised in the jump and ready for action.

The Left-handed Attack. The majority of play in the game takes place with right-handed players. Powerful left-handed players add to deceptiveness in play. Greater attention should be given to the development of the left hand for the attack.

The Distance Attack. This style of attack is a development of recent years. Spikers are coached these days to hit set ups with as much power and deception as possible, regardless of what kind of set up it is. When a ball is set up back from the net, the attack plays the ball by jumping into the air and hitting it with a powerful forward drive, imparting a forward spin on the ball causing a dropping action. Some players face the side of the court and hit the ball with a sweeping overarm, cutting action of the arm. Many of these returns are difficult to handle, especially when the body action is added to give greater power to the attack.

The Second-Play Attack. There is no good reason why the attack should not be made on the second play rather than the third, especially when an easy, lobbing ball comes over the net. Signals should be given to call for such plays. With such a ball the receiver has a splendid opportunity to set the ball for the attack. Usually this set up is made on a diagonal pass to the attack, who should be playing close to the side of the court.

The Fist Attack. The fist is used by many players to hit the ball; however, the majority of players hit the ball with the open hand in order to gain greater control.

The Tap. A tap shot is a spikers' alternative play in which the ball is tapped over the net, relying on accurate placement rather than force. It is particularly effective as a deceptive attack, especially when dropped close to the net. Rigid fingertips hit and direct the ball.

Advance Play Coordination. Each attack player determines with his team mates the kind of set up that is favorable to him. This will vary from a set up that travels 1 or 2 feet above the net to one that reaches 15 feet or more. The beginner should call for a set up that starts to descend when it is 10 to 15 feet above the net. Some spikers like to hit the ball when it is close to the net; others when it is back from it. In advanced play, the high straight set, close to the net, is losing favor owing to the efficiency of the opposing block. A team must be deceptive and ready to vary the nature of its attack, from a slicing smash to a powerful drive made on the second play, or a tap shot.

Two-Foot Take-off Preferred. Be on the alert for the one-foot take-off. This is difficult for the beginner to control. Usually the force of the forward run carries the spiker into the net. This method of approach is like a high jumper's take-off, with the body tipping backward in order to get the hips into the air. In volleyball the attack should be in a forward, tilting position in order to get on top of the ball with greater force.

Straight-Arm Attack. Another fault of beginners is that of using the straight arm for pulling or pushing the ball. Instead of the bent-arm action, the spiking arm is extended upward, and the main power and drive comes from the shoulder. Beginners have little or no power in this form of attack, and in the majority of plays the spiker pushes or throws the ball rather than hitting it.

DRILLS

Practice 1. Jumping Practice. Without using the ball, players should practice spiking stance and jump from the stationary position. Include the spiking arm action after several jumps. After ten trials, the spiker should practice the running approach and attack, using the two-foot take-off.

Practice 2. Warm-up. Warm up the spiking arm by hitting the ball off the hand and driving it down to the floor. Repeat this movement but have the attack jump into the air and hit the ball.

Practice 3. Attack. Have someone stand at the net and toss the ball into the air for the attack to hit. This is of particular value for players who are novices at the skill. A lowered net will aid beginners in learning how to spike the ball.

Practice 4. Spike. The set-up and attack take positions ready to spike the ball over the net. The ball is tossed to the set-up player, who sets the ball up for the attack. This simple controlled exercise will provide an excellent drill for spiking practice. As players advance in skill, the first pass made by the set-up should be a hit rather than a toss.

Practice 5. Hitting. Enclose a volleyball in a mesh bag and suspend it from above with a heavy elastic band. To start the exercise, the bottom of the ball should be about 7 feet 6 inches from the floor. Increase the height as players improve in their timing and jumping ability. Practice hitting the ball, with special emphasis on hitting on top of the ball.

Practice 6. Target. It has been suggested that a spiking rack be built and supported in such a manner that it will also provide a fixed target for the attack to hit. This could be placed close to the net, approximating a game situation.

Practice 7. Downward Drive. Wall spiking has been a standard drill for many years. In this exercise, a player stands about 10 feet in front of a wall with the ball in his hands. He drives the ball forward and downward to a point about 2 feet or more from the wall. The ball bounces forward and upward to the wall and rebounds in an arc, about 10 feet in height, to the attack who jumps into the air and spikes the ball. The downward drive and hitting the ball on top are two major objectives. To score, count the number of times a player is able to hit the ball without letting it hit the floor, other than the drive.

Exercise 8. Block. Spiking against the block. A spiker needs much experience in making the attack against a solid wall of blockers. The best exercise is to practice spiking into two or three blockers for extended periods of time. He should make every effort to outwit the blockers and should learn how to recover balls that have been returned. The only way to learn how to spike against the block is to try deception, placement, cutting, and smashing tactics at every opportunity. Practice game situations provide the best chance for this practice.

Exercise 9. Hand-off Hit. Have one player stand on a chair and hold the ball in a position for normal spiking, close to the net. The spiker hits the ball off the holder's hand. At the instant of contact the holder withdraws his hand.

Exercise 10. Rapid-Fire Spiking. This is an excellent conditioning exercise. The set-up and attack take position at the net. Additional players retrieve and feed a continuous flow of balls to the set-up, who tosses the ball to the attack. After each spike, the attack immediately jumps again and spikes the ball. This is repeated without a rest period. Start with five spikes.

Exercise 11. Quick-Jump Spike. Spiker A takes a position near to and facing the net. An opponent, B, stands 10 feet from the net, facing A. B hits the ball over the net to A, who makes a quick jump and spikes the ball.

TESTS

In the development of the game there has been a lack of valid tests for the attack. The real test comes in actual play, but even here it is difficult to isolate factors that have a bearing on meaningful statistics. The reason, of course, is due to the fact that there are many variants. In addition, the spiker has to deal with a wall of blockers who form another obstacle to conquer. At the present time there is an effort in national tournaments to include spiking results in scoring the game. The following tests are suggested:

VERTICAL JUMP (Sargent Jump). This is one of the standing tests used to note functional ability and may be used in the volleyball program as an indicator of the player's ability to get into the air. It is also an index of general motor ability. The person to be tested stands facing a wall or tall

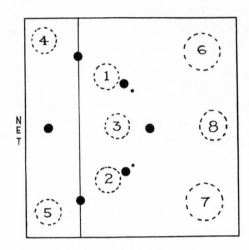

Diag. 24. Nonblocking placement test.

blackboard, with both hands stretched to their limits, chalk having been placed on the tips of the longest fingers. The player makes a mark on the wall with the tips of the fingers. He then turns one side to the wall and jumps into the air, reaching to his utmost, and touches the wall at the highest point of his jump. This marks the upper limits of his jump. The score will be the distance between the lower and upper marks on the wall. Points are scored as follows:

Height (in.)	Points	Height (in.)	Points	Height (in.)	Points
26	100	19	62	13	29
25	94	18	56	12	24
24	89	17	51	11	18
23	83	16	45	10	12
22	78	15	40	9	7
21	73	14	34	8	2
20	67			7	1

NONBLOCKING PLACEMENT TEST. A principle of the attack is to place the ball in the least protected area. For practice in placement, arrange players as illustrated in Diagram 24. This formation is known as the "Half Moon Defense," in which the team on defense forms a semi-circle facing into the attack, with one man playing near the net and directly across from the opposing spiker. This formation is taken when the attack is to be made from the center of the court. For beginners, lower the net to 7 feet 6 inches. The attack player taking the test stands back from the net ready for the ball to be tossed by the teacher. When the ball is tossed, the attack comes forward and

tries to hit the ball into one of the marked areas, between players. The forward areas are most valuable. After ten trials, score as follows:

Attack with speed:

Into Areas:	Points
1 or 2	10
3, 4, or 5	5
6 or 7	1
8	0

Attack·without speed but well placed:

Into Areas:	Points
6 or 7	10
8	5
4 or 5	3
3	1

Repeat this test, using the 8-foot net.

TESTING DURING PROGRESS OF GAME. This is recognized as one of the
best methods of testing the attack. The accompanying attack-scoring chart
may be used to record an attacker's play.

ATTACK SCORING CHART

Name: _____

	Good Set up					Poor Set up						
	Not Over or Out of Bounds	Just Over, Lob	Over with Placement	Over with Speed	Over with Speed and Placed	Not Over, Out of Bounds	Lob	Placed	Speed	Speed and Placed	Net Foul	Line Foul, Over Out of Position
Points	0	0	3	6	8	0	1	5	8	10		
First game												
Second game, etc.												
Total												

ATTACK AGAINST BLOCK. Toss the ball into the air for the attack to play;
at the same time have a player block the ball on the other side of the net.

Score as follows:

Cutting the ball and driving it to the near-side line .... 10 points
Driving the ball by the blocker.................................. 8 points
Placement of the ball, without speed, over blocker's hands or tipping
    ball to the side .... 5 points
Hitting ball into blocker's hands so that it is returned to the spiker   0 points

Repeat the test with two or more blockers.

6

Defensive Play

The first requisite of a good defensive team is that all players must be efficient in blocking and fielding the ball. The unlimited blocking permitted in the 1952 rules brought the art of defensive play into greater prominence as a part of modern power-volleyball. Single, double, and three-man blocks had been permitted at various stages in the development of the game but usually under restrictions. Some teams used the block effectively, but defensive play became more of a science when all restrictions were removed as to the number of blockers and the formations they desired to take. In the early days the attack received priority over defense, and it was conceded that there was little or no defense against an attack of power and speed. This has all changed, and today we find defensive formations in which two, three, four, or more men are sent to the net to block. The block has developed to the point where an opposing attack must be extremely clever, deceptive, and powerful to spike through the blockers. All six men are a part of the defensive effort and must work as a unit, calling for exceptional teamwork.

DEFENSIVE READINESS

All six members of a team must be skilled ball handlers in defensive play. A single weakness will soon be noted by opponents. Failure in defensive play comes from poor skills, lack of confidence, and fear. These may be overcome through constant practice on fundamental play and by the development of the proper attitude. The players who play every ball as though it were the final play of a match exemplify this spirit.

The moment that the ball goes over the net to the opponents, a team goes into a defensive position. Each team member will follow every move of the ball until it is set up for the attack. This will call for speculation as to where the ball is to be hit, by whom, and where it is most likely to go. With every play, the defense studies and shifts into advantageous position. This moving teamwork is brought about through many hours of diligent practice in the fundamental skills and by well-coached team practice games. Let us consider some of the basic skills and requirements for defensive play.

In getting set for defense, the player should have a firm stance, with feet spread and knees bent. The body should be in a crouched position, with hands and arms in front of the head. He should be ready to move quickly to play the ball and to make a dive for it if necessary. The best defensive player is the fast, relaxed type who does not set too tensely but is able to move in any direction instantly. Each defensive player should possess good timing, precise footwork, and speed. He should be able to diagnose what the opposing spiker is planning to do, by watching for tip-offs which he or his team mates discover and disclose. He should be able to jump against the attack at the proper time, following the ball closely with his eyes. Or if he is a non-blocker, he should cover the area for which he is responsible. He should be able to "dig" for low balls and make set ups from any position.

GENERAL PRINCIPLES OF THE DEFENSE

In order to acquire the important skills needed for defensive play, there are several principles which need to be understood and certain techniques which need to be learned.

1. A player should strive to get into the most favorable position so that he can move quickly in any direction to play the ball.
2. He should face directly into the attack and keep his eyes on the ball. Beginners have a tendency to close their eyes or step to one side or to throw up their hands in despair when a smash comes their way.
3. The hands should be raised in front of the chest or the head. This will enable a player to use the head pass to greatest advantage. Or, if the ball is low, he will be able to drop one or both hands for a closed fist or double forearm recovery.
4. A defensive player must study and learn the styles of attack used by opponents. He must move instinctively into the block or court positions for effective defensive play. In addition, he must pass the ball to his team mates in an acceptable manner for offensive play.
5. In view of the present officiating, all defensive players should recognize that they will be penalized for holding the ball if they use the double-open underhand method of recovering the ball. However, when the game is played as a "fun game," as in recreational programs, the following techniques may be used: If the ball is driven so that it falls below the hips, it may be returned by using the double-open underhand pass described in Chapter 3.
6. All players should cooperate with each other, avoiding individual play. Volleyball is a team game and requires the fullest degree of teamwork. In exchange of positions, players assume full responsibilities when they move to play another position. This is especially true when men are required for a blocking formation. They must not interfere with plays by getting in the way.

7. Good footwork is the key to successful defensive play. The player who is quick and light on his feet is the one who seems to have uncanny ability in fielding the ball. Players should condition and strengthen their legs to meet the demands of modern volleyball play.

8. Blocking is now considered to be a standard, effective method of defense. Each player must accept this premise and prepare himself physically and mentally to become an effective blocker.

THE BULWARK OF DEFENSE—THE BLOCK

The dictionary offers a good definition of bulwark. It states that a bulwark is a solid, wall-like, defensive structure. This is exactly what the block is supposed to be. Teams in the far and Midwest deserve credit for the development of the block as an effective defensive play. Coaches who used the block prior to 1952 were faced with restrictions in the number of blockers as well as who could block. Unlimited blocking opened a "new day" for teams on the defense. Successful blocking is now recognized not only as a defensive play but also as a decided advantage in offensive strategy. The recovery of a block presents another chance to play the ball.

In volleyball history the attack has had a definite edge on the defense. Defensive formations were set up on the floor and the spiker had free range in smashing the ball to any position he desired, but this has all been changed. Today the same powerful spiker has to drive time and again in order to get through the block. The effectiveness of the block depends entirely on the effort and time spent in learning blocking skills. With expert spiking, efficient blocking, and recovery, the ball now changes hands several times before a play is completed.

TECHNIQUES OF THE BLOCK. In learning how to block, a novice should practice jumping from a standing position about 18 inches to 2 feet in front of the net. The spring from the floor to get into position for the block is made with both feet. If the block is made close to the net, the body is relatively straight up and down, with the arms slightly tilted forward. Great caution should be taken with beginners to teach them not to bring their arms or hands forward when the block is made, especially if they are close to the net. Doing this usually ends in their going into or over the net.

The player should jump high enough so that his wrists will be in line with and just above the net. This will place his hands just below the spiker's hand. In jumping, the arms should be kept close to the sides or in front of the body, as there will be limited space when two or more block. When the ball is set up for the attack, the blocker should jump in unison with the spiker and closely follow the flight of the ball. In the jump, the arms are thrust upward, elbows straight, bringing the arms together. The hands reach a position about 6 inches from the net, with the wrists in line with the arms.

Diag. 25. One-man block.

The fingers are spread and tilted slightly backward, while the thumbs touch each other to help form a solid block (see Diagram 25).

The correct timing of a block is immediately after the hit, since the spiker will try to drive the ball down. When the spike is made, the fingers tense in readiness for the oncoming ball, which may be deflected backward for further play.

ADVANCED BLOCKING. In modern volleyball it is desirable whenever possible to use the three-man block. This combination, if well coached, can build a wall of six hands and arms, placed close enough together to stop the drives of the attack. A single block will be valuable against a weak spiker, but the single block is not used as a standard play. The double block is more effective, as two clever men can make trouble for most spikers. In addition, there are four men left to cover the court. At times it may be advisable to use more than three blockers, but in general the three-man block is most efficient.

The most important factor in blocking is that of timing. It means following every action of the attack in attempting to discover just where the ball is to be played, when to jump, and where to place the block. It is surprising how efficient a player can become if he sets his mind to the task of blocking. The blocker has an advantage over the attack, since the latter is required to jump higher in order to get on top of the ball for a hit. The blocker's hands are placed below the attack's, with the wrists just above the top of the net (see Diagram 26).

Characteristics of Opponent Spikers. Each blocker must study the various characteristics of all opponent spikers.

Diag. 26. Three-man block.

He looks especially to find:

1. His favorite driving direction.
2. Whether he spikes over the block or through it.
3. Whether he hits a high or low ball.
4. Whether he works with a close set up.
5. Whether he jumps high or low.
6. Whether he gets upset under pressure.

Blocking Tips.   The blocker must be alert on the defense, and immediately following the block, he must bring his arms down in readiness for the recovery of a blocked ball.   His ability in going after low balls and digging them for attack play is important and necessary.

Another essential of good blocking is the ability to move blockers to either side, or the center of the court, in time to make an effective block or to match the opposition if it has faked a play.

In shifting positions, a player must accept additional responsibility for proper court coverage.   Such teamwork brings encouragement and inspiration to his team.   This all adds up to improved morale and better performance.

Blockers should not crowd the net and go over it.

In a three-man block be sure that the fourth man in the front line drops back to cover the court.   He is not to stay close to the net.

The three defensive men in back of the block should be ready and in good position to play the ball.

When blockers come down, they must look immediately for the ball. Blockers' hands should be about a thumb's distance apart and tilted backward.

In a multiple block, the outside player should turn his hands and body slightly toward the court so balls will be deflected into the court.

In backing up blockers in the right half of the court, the left forward drops back and raises his hands.   A half-moon formation is made by having the left back come into the center of the court while the right stays at midcourt filling in the half-moon.

FORMATIONS OF THE BLOCK.   There is no limit to what a team can do defensively if it uses sound fundamentals and displays a determination to recover every ball.   Great emphasis should be placed on the value of quickly moving into the correct position for every play.   The dotted lines in Diagram 27 indicate unmarked divisions of the court.   In subsequent diagrams, two dots will indicate these division points.   Blocking formation is shown by an inverted chevron (**V**).

The One-Man Block 1–2–1–2 Formation (Diagram 27).   One forward player blocks in the center of the court.   The other two forwards take positions along the restraining attack line, 10 feet from the side lines.   The center back moves up to the middle of the court, and the other two backs spread to cover sides and back corners of the court.

The Two-Man Block 3–3 Formation (Diagram 28).   In a two-man block, if the attack is from the right, the center forward and right forward move up to the net to block.   If it is from the left, the left forward will block with the center forward.   If the attack is from the midcourt position, the center forward will indicate which forward he desires to work with.   Much depends on how the play develops.   Many times it is well to have the set-up player block with his attack.   This is particularly effective if teams use the 3–3 system of offense.   The nonblockers move into half-moon formation, the non-blocking forward coming in to protect the blockers on tips, which come over the hands of the blockers.

In the *2–4 formation* (Diagram 29), the left forward and center forward block.   The right forward joins with the other back-field players in forming the half-moon defense, taking a position 5 feet in from the side line and

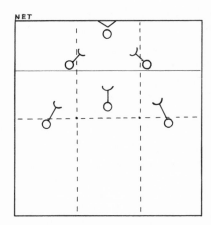

Diag. 27. One-man block, 1–2–1–2 formation, division of court.

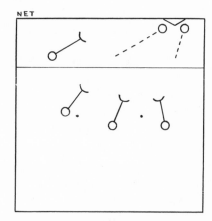

Diag. 28. Two-man block, 3–3 formation.

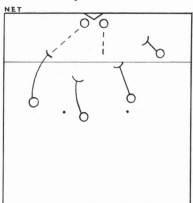

Diag. 29. Two-man block, 2–4
formation.

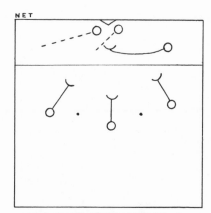

Diag. 30. Two-man block,
2–1–3 formation.

about 7 feet from the net. The right back takes position about 10 feet in from the side lines and 15 feet from the net. The center back moves to a comparable point on the left side of the court, and the left back moves to a position opposite the right forward. Hands are raised as players crouch in readiness to play the ball.

In the *2–1–3 formation* (Diagram 30), two players block and a third backs up the blockers. The center back moves to the center of the court, and the two back wings play 5 feet in from the side lines and 10 feet from the net.

The Three-Man Block. This is a *4–2 formation* (Diagram 31a). This system has been most effective. Four men are responsible for blocking but only three actually do the blocking. It all depends on the location of the attack. If it comes from the right side of the net, the center back moves forward between the right forward and the center forward. If the play is to the left (Diagram 31b), the left forward and center forward move together, and the

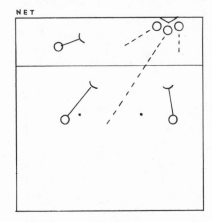

Diag. 31a. Three-man block,
4–2 formation.

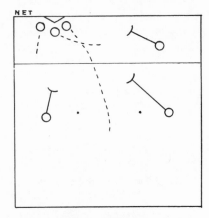

Diag. 31b. Three-man block,
4–2 formation.

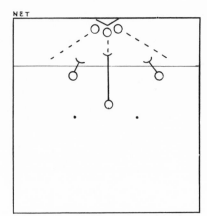

Diag. 32. Three-man block,
3–2–1 formation.

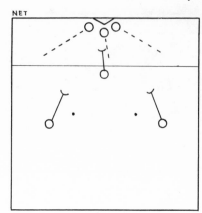

Diag. 33. Three-man block,
3–1–2 formation.

center back comes forward to make the right wing of the block. The two center positions participate in all blocks.

When the block is in place, the remaining players move quickly to guard their areas and to cover the open spots as well as prepare to recover the ball if it gets through the block. Two men cover the back-court areas on each side of the block, and the third man positions himself in line with the attack.

In the block, the center man covers the ball with his hands, the palms facing forward. The two blockers on the sides angle their hands to trap or deflect the ball into the center of the court. The hands are placed about thumbs' distance apart, close enough so as to prevent a ball from going through. The fourth man at the net must be able to get out of the way for subsequent plays.

In the *3–2–1 formation* (Diagram 32), when the three front-line players block, the center back places himself 3 or 4 feet directly in back of the blockers. He will play balls that dribble off the blockers' hands. He also moves up when his team is spiking, to recover balls that are returned.

In the *3–1–2 formation* (Diagram 33), three front players block. One

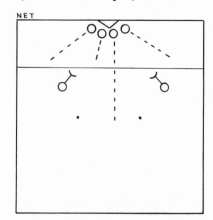

Diag. 34. Four-man block.

player waits for a dropped or deflected ball in the center of the court. The other two cover the corners of the court.

The Four-Man Block (Diagram 34).   In this play the front three men block. The center back moves forward and takes position between the right forward and the center forward. Two center blockers' hands should center on the ball. The right and left backs play midcourt and about 10 feet in from the side lines. This type of block, if well-executed, is hard on spikers who rely on driving power alone, but it leaves much unguarded area to cover. The defensive player must have the ability to properly anticipate the final action of the attack and what happens to the ball when it hits the block. He must be able to retrieve the ball and play it in such a manner that it becomes an opportunity for offensive play.

DEFENSIVE FORMATION

RECEPTION OF THE SERVICE.   When opponents serve the ball, the defensive team should be aligned in the strongest formation possible, for the successful recovery of a serve changes the defensive into an offensive opportunity. Experience has shown that the great majority of serves are placed across the center 15 feet of the court; hence it is good strategy to place the defensive formation in this area.

The player receiving the ball should face directly into its path in a slight crouch, with hands raised to shoulder or head height. He should be ready to shift in any direction in order to follow the course of the ball. On questionable balls, he should call out for the ball. Players should move into the following formation (see Diagram 35a).

The three front-line players move backward to a position across the middle of the court and to the right of their respective areas. The back-

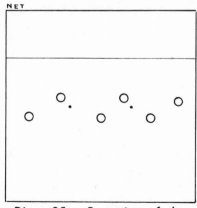

Diag. 35a. Reception of the service.

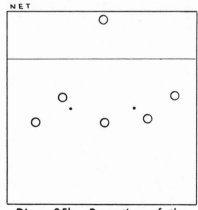

Diag. 35b. Reception of the service.

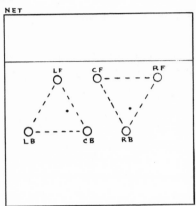

Diag. 36. Double triangle formation.

field players come forward toward the center line, moving to the left and thus forming a staggered line in which the front area men are in front of the three back-field players.

In Diagram 35b, the set-up plays in the center forward area and is in a much better position to handle the ball when it is passed forward. It is advisable to back up the player who receives the serve, especially if the serve is delivered with speed and curve. The right or left back will be in the most favorable position to assist in this play. If the ball goes to either corner of the court, the center back covers the right or left back in order to recover poorly played balls.

V. Hubert Dhanaraj of Madras, India, has written a very helpful text, *Volleyball for Men and Women*. In his book he suggests another defensive formation for the reception of the serve. He calls it the "double triangle formation" (see Diagram 36). Players are staggered so that they do not get in each other's way. Players stand a little to the left so as to take advantage of their right-handedness. In this formation the players are divided to a greater extent in the front-back relationship.

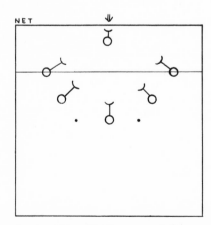

Diag. 37a. Half-moon defense attack at center.

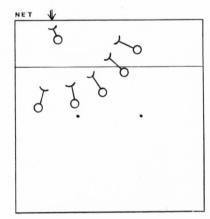

Diag. 37b. Half-moon defense attack from left side.

Major attention has been given to blocking. However, other defensive plays have value.

THE HALF-MOON DEFENSE (Diagrams 37a and b). The general principle of the half-moon defense has been accepted and has given general satisfaction over the years. It is built on the premise that the attack must hit the ball along definite lines of fire. By studying the particular characteristics of players, it is possible to set up an effective defense to meet the attack's offense. As the defense has cupped around the attack, there have been varying degrees of successful returns.

In this form of defense, the players take a semi-circle position, with one forward player forming the pivot or radiating center of the semi-circle (see Diagram 37a). The object of the attack is to smash the ball downward across the court or into the forward part of the court. Therefore, if the defense is set in line of this attack, it will be successful in a sufficient number of times to warrant its use. Diagram 37b shows the positions of the defense when the ball is hit from the side of the court. In this formation it appears that the far corners and back of the court are unprotected areas. Alert defensive action will cover most of the attempts to place the ball in these spots.

Prior to the general use of the block, this formation came in for great use. However, the general principle is the same for nonblockers who, to the best of their ability, move into this formation whether the ball is being blocked or not.

When playing this form of defense, there are two weaknesses which players must guard against. First is the tendency to come too far forward. Continual repetition of this leaves much uncovered territory in the back field, making an easy target for the opposition. The other weakness is that the back line may crouch too low when the ball is hit. Balls will be driven over the hands of the defense if players kneel or bend too low.

DRILLS

Practice 1. A platform is placed on the court adjacent to the net. It should be high enough so that the coach can stand on it and hit the ball to players. Caution should be taken when starting this practice that balls are not hit too hard. Power may be added as players gain in skills and ability to recover balls. Various methods of recovery should be used, including the head pass, fist, back of hand, and double arm.

Practice 2. Teaching defense formations can be an interesting as well as an important part of the training program. The coach should include such drills in every practice period. Merely playing a practice game will never develop the skills and teamwork needed for good play. Diagrams should be posted and explained. The floor should be marked for certain plays, and these plays should be repeated until they become automatic. Each system will have its strengths and weaknesses, and these will show up against different teams. The main objective is to get all members of the team geared into their positions so that they will play the system which has been accepted.

Practice 3. Draw a circle at center point of court; place a defender in position. Spike the ball from the other side of the net and practice recovery of the ball.

Practice 4. Place six men in position on court. Spiker hits ball to men in turn (net is at 7 feet 6 inches).

Practice 5. Player crouches low. Coach, 12 feet in front, tosses ball to player from standing position, who recovers ball and uses closed fist to return it to coach.

Practice 6. Five players form a circle, prepared to play difficult passes. The direction of the ball may be faked or hit hard. Players must be on the alert to recover ball.

Practice 7. Line up three blockers at the center of the net for blocking drill. On the other side of the net, place one set-up and a file of spikers. The three blockers endeavor to block the ball as each spiker in turn tries to drive it through the block.

Practice 8. In team blocking and defense formation, the following drill is to give a team practice in forming the three-man block. Place a set-up and spiker on one side of the net. Team A takes starting position in the opposite court, using four spikers and two set-up players (4–2 system). The attack is made from the left-forward position, which calls for a block to be formed by team A, to the right side of the net. When the play is to the right, the center back moves forward between the center forward and right forward, thus teaming up three men for the block. When the attack is from the other side of the court, the center back moves forward, taking his position in the block, on the right side of the center forward.

7

Offensive Play

Every team should have an offensive system of play which will enable each player to fit into a prearranged plan of action. This coordinated pattern of play should bring about the most effective attack and will require alertness, speed, and drive, as well as the development of strategic movements such as feinting and faking. These deceptive actions have much to do in keeping the opponents guessing and in a quandary as to where and how the ball is to be played by the offense. Advanced offensive play in volleyball calls for increased attention to this department of the game. Today the straightforward smashes and drives of the power spikers are consistently blocked, forcing the attack to time a feint or fake carefully or to use other deceptive movements to draw opponents off balance or to get them out of position. The spiker must have ability to hit the ball with equal force in different ways or directions.

All players must be skilled in the basic fundamentals of handling the ball, and all attack players must be encouraged to master this art. There is no substitute for a well-hit and well-directed pass or set up. The players in the block must be prepared not only to stop the attack but also to play the ball offensively. This calls for clever and alert action on the part of the blockers. Fortunately all players in the block are eligible to play the ball, even the player who clearly hits the ball as the block is made. Setting the ball up immediately following the block is difficult in view of the limited time and space to play the ball. Coming down ahead of the ball and attempting to get into position for a head pass means quick action. If a player is not able to hit the ball with the head pass, a highly coordinated movement is needed to get his closed fist or fists in position for a controlled play.

Players who are backing up the block also must be ready to play the balls that are tipped over the block or lobbed into far corners. Alertness in such plays make up the difference between playing the ball as a scoring opportunity or merely recovering it. Players should have an instinctive reaction regarding the correct handling of the ball from the serve or other plays. Unless the first ball is passed forward properly, other steps in the attack will be more difficult. This is a simple routine but a very important one.

Another cardinal principle of offensive play is to study the positions of opponents, spotting their weaknesses and uncovered floor areas, and learning of their idiosyncrasies. Passing on this information to team mates, especially to the set-up players will place the final attack play in an advantageous position. Attack players must have plenty of fight and determination and must not be discouraged when their spikes are returned time and again by the blockers or by brilliant recoveries.

A spiker who relies on power alone is a poor spiker unless he is able to get over the block. He must be able to mix his shots. There are three basic shots. First is the shot down the near-line that can be hit outside the block or cut off the outside blocker's hands. Second is the shot that can be hit off the tops of the blockers' hands or through a hole in the block. The third shot, which is very effective, is cut off the inside blocker's hands. This ball stays close to the net and is difficult to handle. It is used when the set up is close to the net and the block is close. All these shots are reversed when a player hits the ball from his off-side. The most effective off-side shot is along the near side line.

THE SERVE, AN OFFENSIVE PLAY

A good serve is one of the most effective offensive plays. A player who is able to disturb his opponents with a difficult serve is setting the stage for a returned ball that may result in a score for his team. The tricky, driving volleyball serve is gaining in popularity and may be compared with the tennis serve that comes over the net with placement, speed, spin, and curve. The standard techniques of the serve have been discussed previously in Chapter 4. A player will be rewarded for his efforts in direct proportion to the amount of coaching he receives and the time he spends in diligent practice. New ideas and techniques are being discovered by students of the game, and creative players will continue to develop new methods of making the serve a potent weapon in power-volleyball.

THE SCREEN. A relatively new innovation in play, which favors the server, is a formation of players known as the screen. The object of this formation is to obstruct the view of the opponents by covering the server. Because of this shield, the defense is not able to ascertain the nature of the service. This is especially true when the serve is low and barely skims the net. The rules now permit a freedom of movement as long as the players maintain their order of rotation and the front-line players are stationed in front of the back-line men. Players may move and wave their hands over their heads to aid in the screen. The players take position 10 to 12 feet in front of the server (see Diagram 38). The front-line players stand in close to each other, hands raised. The two back-field players stand in back of them, staggered so as to block the gaps in the front line, thus forming a solid screen.

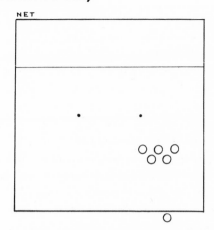

Diag. 38. The screen.

The screen may be moved to any position across the court, in keeping with the server's desires. Three, four, or five men may be used in forming the screen. The screen is particularly effective when the server hits the ball to a particular player or weak formation. Servers develop amazing accuracy in sending the ball to a particular position or person. The men in the screen usually face the net; however, in order to move quickly into a defensive position, a back-field man may face the server and call out a signal when the ball is served. Players then move quickly on this signal to take their places. When opposing teams do not know where the ball is going, they are not able to get set as well for the next play. The server should stand as low as possible so as to take advantage of the screen and to confuse the opposition by hiding the path of the ball.

Limited screens may be formed with fewer than five players. Such formations release players for more efficient court defense.

PLACEMENT OF THE SERVE. The strategy used in the placement of the serve will depend on the defensive formation of the opponents and their weaknesses. If the screen is used, the general principle is to serve the ball to the areas that are protected by the screen. Serves should be made between players rather than directly toward them. Scouting opponents will disclose general characteristics and weak points in their defense.

Serving the ball to the far corners of the court or dropping it over the net and into the front court close to the side lines is usually advantageous. Serves that are driven into the back quarter of the court with dropping action are of value. Servers should be on the alert and should capitalize on players who are out of position.

RECOVERING BALL OFF NET

The ability to recover and pass a ball that has been played into the net is a necessary skill in volleyball. In many instances when it hits the net, the ball seems to hang in the air, thereby giving additional time to play it. Scoring often depends on successful retrieving of such balls.

When the ball is hit into the net, it will rebound and fall differently, depending on the tension of the net and the location of the hit. If it is hit into the bottom section of the net, just above the supporting rope, it will usually pause momentarily. However, if the ball is thrown into the net near the top, it will descend at a rapid rate. This means that the player recovering the ball must move speedily, and it is here that the closed single or double fist may be used. It is advisable for the beginner to use these methods of recovery rather than the double openhand pass. Players should throw several balls into the net to note the reaction of the net. A recovered ball should be passed high enough so that it will be in good position for the attack. Timing is an important factor in this offensive play.

The recovery of blocked balls calls for quick thinking and speedy action. If a person is in the air and the ball falls in front of him, he must drop his hands in order to get under the ball. The closed fist, back of the hand, or double forearm are used to hit the ball. Many times a player will be able to drop on one knee or even roll onto his back in order to use the head pass. This is the most efficient way to handle the ball.

BASIC SYSTEMS OF PLAY (OFFENSE)

THE 3–3 FORMATION (three attack and three set-up). For many years, with but few exceptions, the main offensive system of play was based on the pass, the set up, and the attack, known as the 1–2–3 system of play. A team was organized into three units of two men each, one being called the attack or spiker, and the other the set-up or booster. When a set-up and his attack were in the forward positions, the principle of play was for the set-up to get into position near the net and to await delivery of the ball from any one of his team mates. This first play of the ball is known as *the pass.* Upon reception of the pass, the set-up would then endeavor to set the ball up in such a manner that it would descend to a point most favorable to the spiker. The second play was known as the *set up,* and the third and last play as *the attack.* This 3–3 system of play has been accepted and used for many years. It is an excellent style of play for beginners and is still used by many other teams who have chosen not to use the advanced systems of play.

In Diagram 39a, note the three units, designated as follows: 1–A is the first attack, 1–S is the set-up player for the first attack. White circles indicate the attack players, and black circles signify the set-ups. In this diagram the set-up 1–S, being in the center, is in the most favorable position to receive and set the ball up for his attack 1–A.

In executing this system, players making the recovery and first pass should make every effort to pass the ball high in the air in such a manner that the set-up will not have to move out of his favorable position at the net. He

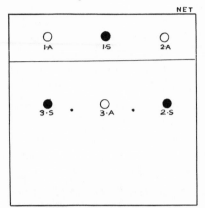

Diag. 39a. The 3–3 system set-up in the center.

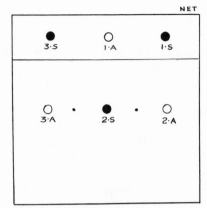

Diag. 39b. The 3–3 system set-up in right-forward position.

should face his attack partner and set up the ball in front of him.   Overcast set ups are difficult to play properly by the attack.

In Diagram 39b you will note that the set-up player 1–S will continue to set up the ball for his attack 1–A.   A very important principle of play in this system is to be sure that players face the person to whom they are passing the ball, except in deceptive action.   It is also imperative that the ball descend in front of a player rather than in back of him.

In the early stages of teaching the game, it is advisable to have the set-up face his team mates and then raise his hands and call for "a good pass."   This will help to center attention on the direction of play.   The importance of this move should be stressed.

When the set-up is playing in the center forward or the right forward position, it is his responsibility to recover all passes.   The only exception to this is when the ball is out of his reach.   This principle of play is important, as there are many situations where other players would interfere if they attempted to play the ball.

Each attack player will have his own ideas as to where and how he wishes his set-up to place the ball for him, and all team members should come to know how best to assist in offensive play.   There is little place for an uncooperative player or one who is easily upset at the net or is perturbed because a team mate has made a poor play.

Knee guards will give protection to players who get down on their knees when playing low balls.   Some players dive for the ball, and some roll into position in order to make a well-placed set up.   The morale of a team is always boosted when a player makes an extra effort to play the ball and score for the team.

The 4–2 OFFENSE (four attack and two set-up).   A new system of play was developed when blocking was strengthened and players were permitted to deliberately shift positions in offensive play.   This new tactic called for four spikers and two set-up players. Front line players were switched, allowing the set up to be made to any location along the net. Experimentation is continuing to improve offensive maneuvers, but it is generally conceded that a team of four spiking threats is the most favorable combination. This system seems to provide the maximum of power and deception while still maintaining an adequate defense.

At present, having six spikers or even five on a team is debatable for general volleyball play, although there are teams using more than four attack men. However, the 4–2 offense has proved its worth. In this formation there are always two spikers in the front line, with the set-ups playing between the two spikers or ahead of them. The main objective is to spread out play at the net, the opposition being kept at a loss as to where the ball is to be played. Deception is essential, and the team controlling the ball should mix up the attack, forcing the defense to scatter their blockers **and never** allowing them to get set in their defensive positions. Here again the set-up and attack must work together to set the ball up for the most advantageous attack.

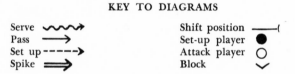

KEY TO DIAGRAMS

Serve	～～～→		Shift position	——(
Pass	——→		Set-up player	●
Set up	-----→		Attack player	○
Spike	⟹		Block	⌄

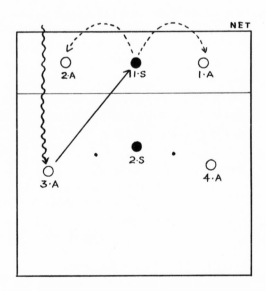

Diag. 40a. The 4–2 system set-
up in center.

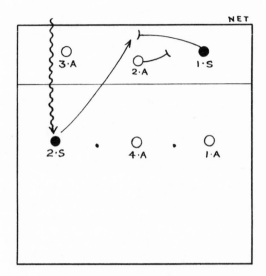

Diag. 40b. The 4–2 system set-
up in right-forward position.

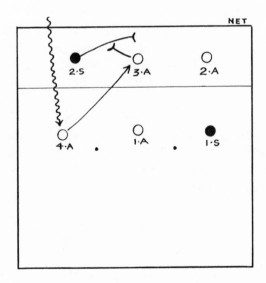

Diag. 40c. The 4–2 system set-
up in left-forward position.

You will note in the accompanying diagrams that the 4–2 system is based
on the shifting of the set-up man to the center of the court whenever he is not
in that position. This places the attack men in the right- and left-forward
positions in all offensive plays.

In Diagram 40a, 3–A receives the serve. He passes the ball to the center of the court to 1–S. 1–S may pass the ball to either 2–A or to 1–A. If 2–A spikes, the other spiker feints to play the ball. If 1–A is to spike, the set-up passes the ball back over his head, while 2–A fakes to play the ball. If 1–A is a stronger attack, the set-up may change positions with him and set the ball for him.

In Diagram 40b, note that there are two spikers together in rotation order. The set-up may play the ball to either of the attack men from the right-forward position or may preferably shift with the center-forward attack and take his place in the center, between the attack men. These shifts make it possible to use the strongest attack player in all three forward positions.

In Diagram 40c, the pass and shift comprise the third formation in the 4–2 offense. Note that the set-up is on the left side of the two attack players. When the ball is served, the left-forward set-up shifts to the center. The center-forward attack moves over to the left-forward position and prepares to attack the ball or feint to hit the ball if it is played to the attack in the right-forward position. However, if 3–A is left-handed, this situation furnishes an excellent opportunity for a power play, especially if the set up is a low-set ball.

THE REVERSE ATTACK. A left-handed player is a real asset in an attack play. Spikers should be trained to hit the ball with either hand. This makes for effective power plays. In Diagram 41, you will note that the ball is passed forward to the left-forward player, who in turn sets the ball up for either the center or right forward, having them hit the ball with their left hand or cut with the right hand.

Additional plays will be presented in the next chapter. Teams should study and adopt a system of play which is practical; overelaborate and intricate plays are valuable only if all six men are able to fulfill the requirements. It is wise to start with a simple fundamental play and then add to this as members increase in individual and team skills.

Diag. 41. The reverse attack.

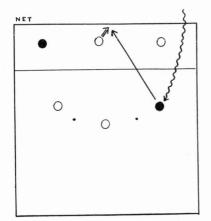

Diag. 42. The two-hit play.

THE TWO-HIT PLAY (Diagram 42). An effective change-of-pace play is known as the two-hit or double play. This is a change from the 1–2–3 attack in that the ball is set up by the player who recovers it from a serve or general play. Many times balls that come over the net with a lob can be handled effectively in this manner. Usually these balls are directed to the back field. When the playing captain notes such a pass, he signals his team by calling out "two," or a similar code call. Such a play usually catches the opponents unprepared. If the defense is ready to block the play, it can always be set up for another attack. The set in this play should have a low arc, being passed just high enough so that if the attack fails to hit the ball, it will go over the net. The attack hits the ball across court, with a tremendous cut. Balls that are dropped over the net and recovered may be played with a low set in which the attack pounces on the ball with a quick smash.

DRILLS

Rapid-Fire Spike. Assemble six volleyballs. The coach stands at the net beside the spiker and tosses the balls up for the spiker to hit. Other players recover the balls and pass them back to the coach, who sets the balls up as fast as the attack can hit them. This is an excellent conditioning exercise.

Calling Plays. Place players on the court ready to receive the serve. The receiving side recovers the ball and plays it according to the play called for by the coach. Review all the regular plays that the team has acquired.

The Fake. The set-ups line up in single file in the center of the court. Attack players form two files, one on the left side and one on the right. The set-up passes the ball to either right or left. The opposite spiker fakes to hit the ball. In making a feint or fake to change the direction of approach, a player, with feet apart, should step forward with one foot and then stop quickly while the body does the feinting. The weight is shifted to the other foot and the attacking approach is made. The spiker makes a lunge step in the other direction and attempts to elude the blockers in his final attack. Faking to hit with one hand and changing the drive to the other is another deceptive play.

Screening Drill. Place men in regular five-man screen formation, with server hitting the ball from the right-back serving area. Have each server make five trials; then rotate the team. Move server to center position and then to the left when all players have had a chance to practice. Targets should be established for the server to hit. Each server should check the positions of men in the screen and make corrections when necessary.

8

Training for
Intensive Competition

A winning volleyball team is the result of physical fitness, basic skills, teamwork, good coaching, and "esprit de corps." Coaches should understand that it will take considerable time to mold a group of players into a smooth-working volleyball team. This is especially true in view of the increasing number of different methods and systems now being developed around the world. In national and international play, volleyball has become an exciting, thrilling game.

Training plans as noted in the earlier chapters of this book should be studied and practiced until they become instinctive. The following are some of the basic elements essential to the development of a team aspiring for top honors.

THE COACH

"To win the game is great,
To play the game is greater,
To love the game is greatest."

This motto, which graces the Hutchinson Gymnasium at the University of Pennsylvania, is most appropriate for all volleyball teachers and coaches, for while winning is a worthy objective, it must be recognized that there are other goals. Our modern Olympics express the thought in this manner: "The important thing in the Olympic games is not winning but taking part." Volleyball needs enthusiastic, intelligent leaders who will motivate others to develop a love for the game. Team morale is a most important factor, as it is based on knowledge of the finer points of the game, competitive spirit, daring, pride of self and team, and a high code of ethics. There is a splendid spirit of sportsmanship in volleyball which every coach and teacher should strive to maintain, for in the development of the game it has been the customary practice for players to call their own fouls in several game situations.

This is especially true when a player touches the net in playing the ball. When such a foul has been committed, the offending player raises his hand and grasps the net, indicating that he has touched it. This is truly the "American Way" of fair play. At times it is impossible for the referee to see such an infraction, and a self-imposed penalty gives an added value to the game.

However, a coach should aim to develop a fighting spirit and a determination to win. He should be an expert and well versed in all phases of the game, especially in the fundamental techniques and the development of offensive and defensive formations. Through scouting, he should be able to analyze the play of opponents and capitalize on their weaknesses and prepare to meet their strong points.

He need be not only a specialist in volleyball but a diplomat as well. He must use the greatest of tact in handling players and understand their various temperaments and dispositions as well as playing abilities. Understanding people requires careful analysis and study. No two men are alike. The coach must know each individual as a person and handle him as such. Some respond to praise and a pat on the back, while others will work best under direct orders.

A coach must take pride in his work and maintain the interest of his players. He should strive to organize and mold his players into a unified, smoothly functioning team. It is up to him to develop a spirit of cooperation and team morale. In this organization he must teach players individual techniques that pertain to each position, and have these merge into well-organized teamwork. The coach should know when to counsel or when to take a player out of the game if he is fatigued, upset, or disgruntled. Such time-outs or substitutions are necessary strategic moves.

The coach should make every practice session a motivating factor in the development of individual play. He should encourage players to take pride in their mastery of skills and team play. Normally, players do not enjoy routine drills and practice formations. This means that the coach will have to keep the practice sessions active and interesting. He must gain the confidence of individuals and the team as a whole. This is acquired through his knowledge of the mental, social, spiritual, and physical background of each of his players. With a sympathetic understanding of these factors, he will come to know what to say and when to do the right thing.

The wise coach will work to keep his players in fine physical condition. This calls for a special effort on his part to impress the men with the need for such conditioning. Today we find a reluctance on the part of the average citizen to go through such a fitness program. Without properly conditioned muscles, a player is handicapped, and his playing ability reduced. He is also subject to strained and sore muscles. If the coach is able to "sell" this program, his efforts will be well rewarded. It is surprising what a difference a month's training program will make in the fitness of any individual. Along with the program of physical activity, a coach should learn of the health habits of his men, including proper diet, proper elimination, sufficient sleep, and a positive frame of mind.

SELECTION OF PLAYERS

In modern volleyball all six members of a team must have a variety of skills. They must be able to set up the ball for the attack; they must be able to block effectively as well as be able to spike the ball.

In building a team, look for the men who show promise as attack players. Select those who are highly developed in skills and playing ability. Fill in the set-up positions with the players who demonstrate ability as the best ball handlers. Every player must have an equal chance to develop his play. The wise coach will see to it that each player's progress is noted and attention is given to improving his play. Progress is made in the fire of competition. Careful study of an individual's play will reveal his potential as a team member. Players must have an opportunity to demonstrate ability under game conditions.

Basic qualifications of the set-up and the attack are considered in the subsequent paragraphs.

THE SET-UP. A set-up should be athletic, quick, alert, versatile, with particular ability to receive and pass the ball. On the defense, he must be prepared to run or dive after the ball and play it safely to another team mate. His hands and arms should have unusual strength and dexterity to control and pass the ball. The set-up is the key to all successful scoring plays in that his accuracy in placing the ball for the attack must be developed to pinpoint efficiency. In addition to setting up the ball, he must be ready to move into the formation of a block or switch positions at the net as the team strategy demands. All things being equal, the taller the player, the greater the effectiveness, for height helps in blocking and gives greater range in defensive play.

A set-up must anticipate where the ball is to be played and then move into the best position for recovery of the ball. He must have a single purpose and determination to go after every ball that is hit to his respective area. If the ball fails to come to that spot, he must be ready to fit into the next best defensive position and be ready to back up other players. Cooperation with the attack calls not only for playing ability in placing the ball exactly where the spiker wants it, but it also requires an understanding of the disposition and idiosyncrasies of that person. A set-up must encourage the spiker when opponents are making it difficult for him to get the ball across the net. When an attack is irritated, the set-up must be understanding and use diplomacy in bringing him back to emotional stability. A set-up should recognize that his position is one in which there is no so-called glory. The spiker is the person who gains the plaudits of the crowd when he smashes or drives the ball through the opponents. Fortunately there is an increasing recognition of the contribution of the set-up players.

THE ATTACK. The requirements of the attack call for an extended list of qualities, which have been discussed in the chapter on the attack. As in basketball, height is of great importance. This is especially true when it comes to blocking and in getting the ball over or through the defense. A spiker must have great stamina, powerful legs, and arm action that is able to smash, cut, or drop the ball. He must be able to block effectively, pass and set up the ball, serve, and cover his area in defensive play.

He must be an expert in deceptive play, faking to hit the ball, switching and shifting positions, ready to fit speedily into developing plays. He must be able to decipher the opponents' plan of attack and move into the correct defensive position. He not only should attack effectively in the front of the court but also while he is playing the back position.

The spiker should be ready to take advantage of a low set with a fast jump and spike. He must be quick to hit the ball directly from the pass or take advantage of a good set up made by a mistake on the part of the other team. He should study the play and floor positions of opponents, looking for open spaces and weaknesses in defense. An attack should be able to jump into the air and reach at least as high as 9 feet 6 inches.

CONDITIONING

The coach faces a real problem in the care of his men away from the volleyball court. He must motivate them to take a sincere interest in their physical and mental fitness in order to play winning volleyball. The importance of this factor can be discussed at a meeting arranged away from the playing court. The group should discuss and agree upon a system of training that they would be willing to follow. The following topics are offered for consideration.

THE CONDITIONING PROCESS. Inactivity means flabby muscles. Body tone is built when we extend ourselves. A training program is necessary if we wish to condition our bodies for efficient action. The following exercises will do much to bring about physical fitness. The wise coach will be aware of the fact that such a routine is not a popular one with the average volleyball player because he wants to "get on with the game." Some of the more common exercises are:

1. Running—in or out of doors; excellent for legs and endurance.
2. Skipping—indoor; lengthen strides for stretch.
3. Rope Skipping—interesting and beneficial.

4. Full knee bends.
5. Assume squat position; lean forward and rest weight on finger tips. Shift weight back on legs, move fingers forward, rest weight on tips, continue to full leaning rest position.
6. Face wall, stand arms' distance from wall, lean forward, place weight on fingers, push back, step back, and repeat, each time placing greater weight on fingers.
7. On back, face up, arms over head; sit up and touch toes.
8. Squat, extend legs back, jump forward to squat, stand.
9. Practice three-step attack jump (left, right, left, together, jump).
10. On back, face up; lift both legs, let down on three counts.
11. On back, feet spread; sit up, move right hand to left foot, return to floor, sit up, left hand to right foot.
12. Squat position, use duck waddle across or around the gym.
13. Stand, feet astride, hands behind neck; side body bend left, then right.
14. Same with hands overhead, bend sideward .
15. Coaches are utilizing the weight-lifting program these days to increase the power of the legs. When weights are available, players use them in the knee-bend exercise by placing the bar across the shoulders and repeating the exercise. Individual work-outs between practice periods are advisable. Use of pulley weights, mat exercises, medicine ball drills, running and jumping are excellent to maintain fitness. Warming-up periods prior to a game should be of short duration, approximately 5 minutes.

HEALTH HABITS. Players should take pride in their ability to maintain good health. The health habits of players vary. The coach should learn from each player certain facts that have a bearing on the mental and physical fitness of his players.

He will work closely with these players in the development of a satisfactory program. Nutrition is of great importance. Players should recognize the place of a balanced diet. The essentials suggested in the McCullom foundation diet form a sensible program. This includes eggs, butter, cheese, milk, fruits, and green and yellow vegetables. If a player is carrying too much weight and is gaining, he should consult his physician. Incidentally, a wise coach will keep track of the weight of his squad. Post a weight chart on the wall near the scales. Players should never overload their stomachs before play. At least three hours should elapse between a meal and play. This time may be shortened if a light meal of tea, toast, and eggs is served.

Eight hours sleep is necessary for most men. Players should avoid worry and tension as much as possible. Emotional stability is a cardinal virtue and is a direct factor in the ability to live a normal life.

Liquor is taboo. It has no place in competitive volleyball. Excessive tobacco smoking is a detriment to volleyball players in view of the strenuousness of the game.

SELECTION OF A SYSTEM

The coach is responsible for the selection of systems of play. It is also his responsibility to see to it that the players thoroughly understand them. This calls for many "blackboard sessions" and much drill on the floor to become familiar with these plays. Introductory sessions give players an opportunity to ask questions and to make suggestions. Dinner meetings have special significance in a team-building program, and they help to build morale. When final decisions are made, they become the accepted policy of operation in which all players have had a chance to express themselves.

Systems should be built as much as possible on the abilities of the players. It may be necessary to start a season with the 3–3 system rather than the 4–2. Or a team may select the six-spiker system. It is advisable for teams fighting their way up to persevere with a simple system rather than try razzle-dazzle play.

With a good average team, a coach will be wise to select the 4–2 system of offense with four spikers and two set-ups. This gives a flow of power at the net and permits deception and opportunity for changing formations. On defensive play, the strongest combination seems to be the system that calls for four eligible men for blocking, with three actually making the final block. In screening the serve, five men or less may be used effectively.

In designing a system of play, a coach should devise a code of signals, utilizing words, hands, or numbers. The signals should be simple and easily recognized. Complicated signals are not easily grasped and may cause more confusion than verbal direction.

On the defense, signals may call for the number of blockers to be used in the block. However, prior to the game, the coach usually indicates the number of blockers to be used against each of the opponent spikers. He may use four blockers against a driving spiker or two against a weaker attack. It must be kept in mind that with the swift development of play, there may be little time for signaling. Once a system has been selected, it is important for the coach to strive for improvement, capitalizing on the strengths of his players.

TEAMWORK

Having good players and a system of play is important, but unless there is teamwork, a team will be handicapped from playing its best game. Team spirit and morale make the difference between an average or a winning team. Teamwork is the result of careful planning and a series of practice sessions, but a good coach who encourages and inspires his players is just as important. He must develop confidence and fire his players with a determination to win. Teamwork calls for a positive mental attitude among team mates.

The real test of team play is in working with and supporting other fellow players in a game. Having an appreciation and knowledge of what the other players can and are going to do is essential; for example, moving to the right side to form a three-man block, with the remaining players covering for a returned ball. This calls for the center back to move forward between the right and center forwards, thus forming a three-man block and leaving the left forward and the two back men to form the defense. When each man knows the others by his side, there comes a feeling of team play and support for each player. To be able to team with a partner or two so that the combination presents a well nigh impenetrable barrier to a spiker, or to be a part of a deceptive play at the net, is a real accomplishment.

Team play is broken when a player runs at will to various parts of the court. His dashing into a team-mate's area is disturbing and detrimental to any system of play. If a player fails in his assignment and continues to do so, it will not be long before opponents locate this weakness and take advantage of it. Participants must take extra precaution not to interfere with other players in close work such as blocking, spiking, or the screen. In blocking there are many hazards that may cause injuries; keeping the elbows out to the side and thereby jabbing into team mates; or spreading the feet on return to the floor and thus risk turning an ankle.

Each player must learn the weaknesses and strengths of his team mates. He must learn how to protect the weak points and take advantage of the strong ones. Team strength cannot be built on the work of the star alone. Every member of the team must always be alert to perform his job to the best of his ability. Players should never develop a fear of any play of the opponents—or of their own ability to play the ball properly. They should have the spirit of the wildcat in readiness to pounce into any play with force and determination. Team play requires careful planning and much practice in order to secure perfect coordination of all players.

PRACTICE SESSIONS AND PRACTICE GAMES

GENERAL PRINCIPLES. It must be clearly understood that it will take considerable time to build a team. Some coaches and teachers feel that it is necessary to spend 60 hours in fundamental techniques and team practice before a group will begin to assume the teamwork stage.

The basic requirements of the two types of play (namely, offensive and defensive) have been discussed previously. The importance of teamwork in developing a winning volleyball team has also been stressed. Procedures in the development of team play will now be discussed.

Practice in Fundamental Techniques. The mastery of fundamental techniques will call for a carefully worked-out plan of procedure. A coach should outline a series of drills and exercises that will not only improve individual play but will also retain the interest of all members of the squad.

Serving, passing, spiking, blocking, screening, getting the ball off the net, recovering drives, and smashes are techniques that usually need to be improved upon. Drills in these fundamentals need to be presented continuously throughout the season, with extra attention being given to the art of service. While players are practicing these fundamentals, the coach and his assistants should be on the alert for weak points in performance. They should never let players get careless or start to "play around with the ball."

Plenty of volleyballs should be available for these practice sessions. In early season it would be well to spend at least a half-hour in such drills.

Testing and Rating Players. The wise coach will keep records on each of his players. These grades or test results will help to keep him informed so that he can be more helpful in improving individual play. Every player should be given the Brady test when the season starts. Occasional retests should be given to note progress in passing ability. Serving tests will indicate player ability in placement of the serve. Spiking tests will indicate whether or not a spiker can hit the ball to specific targets. Each coach will develop his own tests to suit the needs of his players. The best grading will take place when players are graded on team performance during actual play. The coach should have records on a player's serve, his passing efficiency, his effectiveness as a spiker, and his ability in recovering difficult plays. He should carefully work out an evaluation of these findings and discuss them with the players involved. Testing takes time, but it produces much valuable data.

Blackboard Sessions. During the early season it is well to hold a meeting of all players to discuss systems of play and to come to final agreement on points where there is a difference of opinion. Dinner meetings seem to furnish the best atmosphere for such a gathering. Movies and special volleyball authorities can be presented, or a volleyball expert can expound on special systems of play or other volleyball topics. It is well to let your players have an opportunity such as this, in order that they come to feel that they have a share in the planning and over-all teamwork of the group. Weaknesses in individual and team play can form the basis for a lively discussion on how to improve the situation.

The Practice Game. Be sure that players are properly warmed up before they go into practice or competitive play. During early season, play will be ragged for many reasons: players may not be in the best physical condition, fundamental techniques may not have been mastered, or players may not know one another. It is advisable to utilize the 3–3 style of offense for the first week or so until the players become accustomed to working together. Teams that hold over from season to season need not revert to the simpler system but can continue to use the previous season's style and system of play.

As players develop, they should be shifted into positions of greatest value, thereby enabling a coach to integrate his forces for the maximum efficiency. Shifting and moving players is a difficult assignment at times, especially in view of the enthusiasm of players to make the first team.

It is important that the best combination of players be selected as soon as possible. Scrimmage between first and second or third squads can be beneficial if properly supervised. Practice games should be conducted with good officiating. In fact the referee should call infractions most critically, not allowing any laxness in play, especially in holding the ball.

The coach should stop play when a mistake or error has been made and explain or question players as to why such a misplay was made. It is well to have the players gather around the coach for such discussions, even though it may slow down the game. If a practice game becomes listless, it would be well to shift into other forms of practice or call it off.

Practice Scrimmage. To practice continuously with the same players tends to break down morale unless both teams have equal abilities and the games are enthusiastically played. Even with such ideal conditions, it is well to invite other teams to participate on a practice basis. During such sessions coaches are permitted to stop the game and discuss with their players mistakes and suggestions for improved play. They are permitted to coach from the side lines at all times. During the last stages of such a match, coaches may find it advisable to operate on a regular basis of play, except for time-outs to discuss or instruct. Such practice is an ideal situation for the development of team play. These games furnish an opportunity for grading players and give much valuable material regarding the abilities of players.

VARSITY PLAY AND SCHEDULES

SCOUTING. Scouting is a part of modern athletics. It is a special effort to study opponents' strategy, systems of play, strengths, and weaknesses. An analysis and interpretation of these findings should help a coach to prepare his team to center attention on combating strengths and capitalizing on weaknesses. Here are some of the items that should be included in such a scouting program:

1. Starting line-ups of opponents.
2. Charts to diagram offensive and defensive plays.
3. Defensive formations and tactics used in blocking. What system: 2, 3, or 4 blockers, or more. Who are the weak defensive players. How the team members hold their hands. Who blocks and who covers back field. Open spaces in court when blocking.
4. For the offense, note the type, whether a screen is used and with what effect. Are the set ups deceptive with clever faking by one or more players. Who are the most effective spikers.

5. Note serving ability, kinds of serves and placement, low, high, floater, spin, trick, or drop.
6. Reception of the serve; note weaknesses. Note most effective serve against opponents.
7. Check the attack players. Note favorite position to spike; where the set up is made, close to the net or otherwise. High or low set. How the attack is executed and the favorite angle of spike.
8. How is their composite spirit and teamwork; how do they stand up under fire.
9. Other miscellaneous thoughts: Best method is for the coach to scout. Coach should watch opponents in warm-up periods and secure characteristics of each player.

PLAYING THE GAME. A team should go into competition fired with a determination to win and to play every ball as though the game depended on the results of that effort. This enthusiasm should come from the final words of the coach, whose encouragement and inspiring spirit instill in each player a desire to give his best. A smooth-working team does not require a raving, threatening tirade. The grip of the hand and the pat on the back carry significant meaning. However, enthusiastic encouragement is an important factor in team morale.

The playing captain carries the responsibility for leading the team while it is on the floor. His assignment is an important one, especially in keeping team members pulling together. He must calm players who become upset because of errors or mistakes, and he should never let a team member argue with the officials when he feels that they have made a mistake. This is the captain's responsibility.

If the team is winning, a coach should do everything in his power to keep them in this frame of mind. He should keep pressure on his players never to slow down when they are ahead. Too many games have been lost through a team's over-confidence in their lead. In tournament play a team should be coached to face every opponent with but one objective, namely, to win. Until the game and match are over, every play should take on vital meaning. The coach should not break up a winning combination in order to give others a chance to participate. This seems to be a brutal stand to take, but if a team desires to win, no changes should be made unless they strengthen team play. Breaking up a winning combination does harm to the players' morale and may upset organization and power of play.

All members of the squad want to play at every opportunity, but if the group has the proper team spirit, they will remain on the bench and glory in the good work of the six men who, through the efforts of the total squad, have reached a stage of proficiency. On the other hand, it is important that the coach should take every opportunity to keep the substitute in good spirits. Substitutions, to give players a rest or to counsel or to relieve a player of extreme tension, are valuable and should be made as necessary.

When opponents make a run of points against a team, the playing captain or the coach should call for a time-out. He should bring his team together and quickly note the weaknesses and offer instructions to overcome them. This is another time for encouragement. Do not leave the players to themselves when time-out is called; join with them.

It is well to have oranges, lump sugar, or possibly dextrose to give to players between games and matches. These build quick fires for energy and refresh men under strain.

Players should be encouraged to play a clean game and to call net-touching fouls. Taking advantage of weaknesses in play is legitimate, but volleyball calls for a consideration of the rights of opponents. The attitude toward officials and their decisions should be positive. The wise coach will take occasion to compliment officials and will coach his players not to lose their tempers over decisions which seem to them to be wrong.

Modern play calls for power and tricky serving. The days are past when a safe, easy serve was the order of the day. Teams should be coached to serve the ball with deception and power in an effort to make it impossible for opponents to return. Steady improvement is being made in this department of the game. More "english" is being used, and the ball is being hit harder in many different ways.

A coach should inspire the team to secure as many points as possible in the early stages of the game. They are easier to get at this time. This means that extra pressure must be directed to a team when a new game gets under way. Trick plays may be used when a team is working well. When things are not going well or a team is off balance, such plays are rather risky.

Be sure that the team plays the accepted system, either on the defense or the offense. Deviations should be taken only when other team members are informed and know what to do. Lazy players who are not responding should be eliminated from the game, for they make it possible for opponents to spot them and play on their weaknesses.

Keeping your players at a high pitch requires great insight and understanding of people, a sense of humor, and faith in fellow men. Schedules are heavy and details are many, but when a team is pulling together, all the hours of hard work are amply rewarded.

THE SCHEDULE

A schedule will depend on your location and the availability of volleyball teams. In some sections of the country the game has been included in interscholastic and intercollegiate schedules. However, the game has not received financial support as much as other games. This means that travel is limited, and the schedule depends on the interest and financial status of players and friends. With YMCA and club teams, there are many more opportunities for play, especially in YMCA circles, where the game has been recognized and supported.

Long auto trips are expensive and time-consuming. When it is possible to travel by air, bus, or train, expense limits the amount of traveling that can be done. Major national tournaments continue to attract the best teams across the country in spite of the expense of travel. Funds for these trips are usually raised by the teams involved. Travel to international points is paid by individual players.

A schedule should be built with weaker teams starting the season. These games may be used to smooth out team play and to gain experience in special tactics or strategy. Early victories assist in building morale. For college and club teams two matches per week makes a good schedule. Tournaments give greater chance for extended play. One major tournament or match a week would be satisfactory for club or college play. Most of the major tournaments are held on Saturdays, when 4 to 16 teams are invited in for play.

9

Officiating

As in other sports, there is a great need for good volleyball officials. These officials must be able to control and direct the game in such a manner that coaches, players, and spectators are unaware of their presence. This is quite different from referees who make the game center around themselves. There are many plays and situations in volleyball that call for split-second decisions and judgments, especially play at the net and proper handling of the ball. Fortunately the officials are aided by having players call their own fouls at the net.

Officials must be familiar with the rules, understanding them thoroughly, and be able to interpret them satisfactorily. They should keep up to date by having copies of the latest volleyball official guides.*

DUTIES OF THE OFFICIALS

REFEREE. The referee is the superior official of the game. He takes position on a platform at one end of the net so that he can clearly see both courts. His head should be above the net, at least 2 feet and not more than 3 feet. He has power to overrule decisions of other officials when, in his opinion, they have made errors. He decides when the ball is in play, when it is dead, when a point is made, and when penalties occur. He has power to make decisions on any questions not specifically covered in the rules. In protests regarding interpretations, he checks all details relating to exact positions of players, time, score, and nature of the protest before permitting the game to proceed. Time-outs and substitutions may be requested from either the referee or the umpire. He declares a time-out when an injury has occurred.

UMPIRE. The umpire takes a position on the opposite side of the court from the referee. He makes decisions on crossing the center line below the net and keeps the official time of time-outs. He keeps account of the time

---

* *Volleyball Official Guide,* published by the USVBA, Men and Women. Also *Volleyball Guide,* published by the American Association for Health, Physical Education and Recreation Division for Girls and Women's Sports (DGWS).

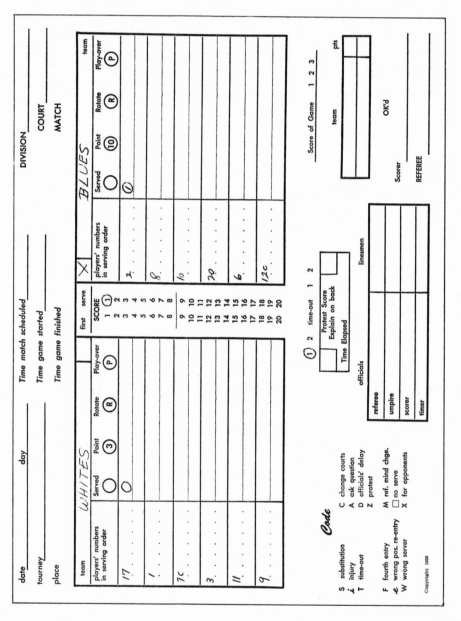

Diag. 43. Volleyball score sheet (USVBA).

allowed for injuries and time between games. He may authorize substitutions and time-out requests in place of the referee. He also assists the referee in calling violations of unsportsmanlike conduct of players, players out of position, or helps in any other way requested by the referee. Recent rulings now permit the umpire to move from his former position "under the net" to either side. He should stand in a location that enables him to be in the best position to observe play without interfering.

The umpire has a very important position, especially if the referee requests his aid in calling fouls and errors made in net play. He should watch the receiving team on the serve, checking respective positions. He should have a differently toned whistle than the referee. He should be alert to calling fouls on players who touch the bottom of the net with any part of their body. He calls violations involving player conduct, such as stamping of feet, yelling at a player when he is about to play the ball, or making derogatory remarks about, or to, opponents or officials.

SCORER. The scorer keeps the official record and score of the game. He is seated beside the umpire and opposite the referee. He has jurisdiction for the operation and control of the official scoring devices and records. He records the points as indicated by the referee. The scorer secures the names and numbers of the starting players and their serving order, indicating who is to serve first, after the choice of serving has been determined. The scorer is not permitted to disclose the line-up of one team to the other. He should take special care in noting the rotation order of each team and see to it that teams maintain this order. If a player is out of position when a serve has been made, or as soon after as possible, the scorer informs the umpire which player is out of position. He keeps the record of the number of time-outs for rest and substitutions. He records the substitutions made. During the third game of a match, he directs teams to change courts at midgame, when one team has scored eight points, or when the ball is dead after 4 minutes of play.

The scorer is responsible for keeping spectators informed as to the score. Well-placed electric scoring and timing boards are good investments. When a match is completed, the scorer secures the signatures of the referee, signs the score sheets, and turns them in to the court or tournament chairman.

A scorer checks all time-out periods taken by teams. He indicates whether the time-out was requested for rest or substitution. Teams are permitted two rest periods per game; a third constitutes a violation.

Diagram 43 is the current score sheet that has been developed by the USVBA and is highly recommended for tournament use.

TIMEKEEPER. The timekeeper is seated on the side of the court opposite the referee and near the scorer. He operates a suitable timing device, keeping a record of the time the ball is in play. He starts the clock the instant the ball is hit on the serve and stops it when the ball is grounded or an official blows his whistle. If no visible timer is available to indicate remaining time, it is the duty of the timekeeper, when the ball is dead, to call out in a loud voice the number of minutes left to play: "4," "3," and "1."

While the duties of the timekeeper are not difficult, they are extremely important. He should be alert to start and stop the clock when time is in or out. He calls the game when 8 minutes have elapsed and one team has a two-point margin. If the two-point margin does not exist, he lets the game continue without interruption until one of the teams has gained this two-point lead.

The rules indicate that at midpoint in the third game of a match, the referee directs teams to change courts. To indicate this midpoint, the time-keeper sounds his whistle the first time the ball becomes dead after 4 minutes of play. It is important that the timekeeper does not stop play until the ball is dead.

THE LINESMEN. Two or four linesmen post themselves outside the corners of the court, watching the assigned court lines. With two linesmen, two lines will have to be observed; with four linesmen, each will have but a single line. The linesmen are responsible for calling any serving fouls. A linesman blows his whistle and indicates to the referee when a server steps on the serving line or touches the floor outside the serving area. The linesmen follow the play of the game, with special reference to balls touching on or outside of the boundary lines. The use of hand signals will indicate whether the ball touched the line or not. If it touches the line, it is indicated "safe"; if outside, "out."

The linesman also has another assignment. He is responsible for noting whether the ball passes outside the vertical marker on the net, above the side lines, and when the ball hits the net outside the vertical marker. He notifies the referee when these infractions have been made. The nearest linesman to the server takes charge of the ball when time-out has been called. He returns it to the server when the referee resumes play.

It is a common fault for linesmen to become distracted at times from their duties. This is especially true when a linesman is requested to officiate in more than one match in succession. Caution should be taken to have sufficient linesmen in attendance to keep this important point of officiating as efficient as possible. Linesmen may also be helpful in keeping spectators from getting onto the court or passing in back of the courts and interfering with play.

DEFINITIONS OF TERMS *

Own Court. Opponents' Court. The court occupied by a team is called its own court; that occupied by the opponents, the opponents' court.

* *Volleyball Official Guide*, 1960 (USVBA Printer).

The Net. Any part of the net, whether it is over the court or not, is to be included and officially recognized as a part of the net when players touch it. The supporting cables and ties are also "in play." This means that players are not allowed to touch any part of the net or supporting cables while the ball is in play.

Serving Order. The order in which the members of each team are to serve.

Position. When a serve is made, all players must be in their respective rotation positions: all front line players in front of all backline players. Any part of a player's body touching the floor may not overlap any part of another player's body.

Rotation. The shifting of players in a clockwise manner is called *rotation*.

Service. A service means putting the ball into play by the player in the right-back position, who hits it over the net into the opponents' court with the open hand, fist, or arm while standing in back of the end line of the court.

Point. A "point" is called when the receiving team fails to return the ball to the serving team.

Side Out. A side out is called when the serving team fails to win its point or plays the ball illegally.

Dead Ball. The ball is "dead" after "point," "side out," or any other decision temporarily suspending play.

Playing the Ball. A player who touches the ball or is touched by the ball when it is in play is considered as playing the ball.

Out of Bounds. The ball is out of bounds when it touches any surface or object or the ground outside the court.

Catching or Holding the Ball. A held ball is ruled when the ball comes visibly to rest at contact. The rules indicate that a ball must be clearly hit.

Dribbling. A player touching the ball more than once with any part of his body is considered as dribbling.

Blocking. Blocking is a defensive play close to the net in which players attempt to intercept the ball as it crosses the net. Raising a hand or hands over the head constitutes an attempt to block.

Error. An "error" is a failure to play the ball as permitted under the rules. There are five main violations classified as errors:

1. Holding or throwing the ball.
2. Hitting ball twice in succession (dribble).
3. Taking more than three plays to get ball over net.
4. Serving ball into net or out of court.
5. Playing ball into net or out of court.

Foul. A foul is an encroachment of the rules and takes precedence over an error when committed on the same play.

A Play. A play is the action of a player or players contacting the ball, including preliminary action and following movements to regain equilibrium. Action of a spiker and blockers constitutes a single play. Plays may often overlap one another.

Play-over. A play-over is the act of putting the ball into play again, by the last server, without awarding a side out or point.

Screening. Screening is an attempt by players on the server's side to hide or screen the serve.

Simultaneous Contacts. Simultaneous contacts are contacts made at the same instant.

Spiked Ball. A spiked ball is one that is hit with force over the net.

IMPORTANT RULES *

A summary of the most important rules is given in the following list:

1. The court is 30 by 60 feet and the top of the net is 8 feet high (for women, 7 feet 4¼ inches).
2. To start the game, the referee tosses a coin to determine which team gets the choice of court or serve.
3. A team must have six players in order to play a game. When it is reduced to less than six players, the game is forfeited.
4. A team serving first yields the starting service of the next game.
5. In serving the ball, the server stands in back of the end line and between the side lines.
6. Members of the team serve in turn, the server continuing to serve until side out is declared.
7. It is a foul when the server steps on the end line in making a serve.
8. It is not a foul to step on the center line, but it is a foul to go over it.
9. Touching the net with any part of the body is a foul except when the ball is driven into the net, causing it to hit an opposing player.
10. Reaching over the net is a foul, except when the net is driven under a player's hand by opponents.
11. It is an error to catch, lift, push, or throw the ball. The rules distinctly state that it must be batted.
12. It is an error to hit the ball twice in succession.
13. Points are scored only by the serving team.
14. Three plays are allowed to get the ball over the net. Four plays constitute an error.
15. If the ball touches a boundary line, it is counted as good.

* *Volleyball Official Guide,* 1960 (USVBA Printer).

16. A game is won when a team has scored 15 points and has a two-point advantage. In tournament play, 8 minutes of ball-in-play-time is added. In this case a game ends when a team scores 15 points before the time expires or at the end of 8 minutes, regardless of the score, providing a team has a two-point advantage. If a team does not have a two-point advantage, play continues until one team has a two-point advantage.

17. Back-field players are not permitted to spike a ball close to the net. However, they may spike a ball on or in back of the 7½-foot restraining line.

18. Teams shall change courts at the end of each game. In case of a third game, teams will change courts at the midpoint of the game.

19. When a serve has been made, players are free to move to any position in their court.

20. A player may use any part of his body to play the ball except when he is serving; here he may use his hand, fist, or arm.

21. A player may return to a game twice but only in his original line-up position.

22. A ball may be recovered from the net except when it is a served ball.

23. All six players may block on the same play.

24. When the ball is served, players on both teams must be in their rotation order, with forward players in front of back-field players and no overlapping of feet forward or sideward.

25. When a foul and error are committed in the same play, the foul takes precedence.

OFFICIALS' SIGNALS

A set of signals has been developed over the years to assist in officiating a game. Diagram 44 furnishes sketches of these signals:

1. **Point.** Raise right arm and point index finger upward.
2. **Side Out.** Point right hand toward serving team on right; point left hand toward serving team on left side.
3. **Time-out.** Form a "T" with both hands.
4. **Double Foul.** Cross arms in front of chest.
5. **Over the Net.** Place hand over net and point toward offending team.
6. **Touching the Net.** Grasp net and point to offending team.
7. **Crossing Center Line.** Palm up under net cable; point to offending team.
8. **Out of Position.** Place both hands on hips.
9. **Double Hit.** Hold up two fingers.
10. **Four Hits.** Hold up four fingers.
11. **Thrown Ball.** Two sweeps of right arm over head.
12. **Held Ball.** Flex arms, palms up, flex fingers two times.
13. **Lifted Ball.** Slowly raise both hands in a lifting motion.
14. **Technical Foul.** Cross arms on chest.
15. **Linesmen's Signals**
    a) Ball in: both hands raised forward with palms down.
    b) Ball out: raise both arms and point thumbs over shoulders.

Diag. 44. Official's signals.

HINTS ON OFFICIATING

GENERAL PRINCIPLES OF OFFICIATING. The referee must have a complete knowledge of the rules. It will be necessary to study them constantly, for a mistake in interpretation is unpardonable. It is also important that he maintain friendly relations with the players without becoming too familiar. He must keep the game under control at all times through his strictness and not by domination. He should encourage players to call their own fouls at the net, through an attitude of appreciation for this help. The nature of intensive play at the net is such that there are many plays which cannot be called accurately without aid. This is essentially true when only slight contact has been made by one or more players at the net. This honor system makes it possible for the game to be called far more accurately and fairly.

Every referee makes decisions instantaneously and utilizes the hand signals to indicate the nature of the infraction. He should have a clear understanding with other officials so that his decisions will not conflict with theirs. He must not permit bickering or unseemly conduct to continue in the game. Some players seem to take special delight in objecting to officials. Their attitude is negative. Overwrought players belong on the bench and not in the game. The expert referee will not antagonize players but will do everything in his power to keep the players' attention on the game and not on the officiating. Officials should firmly believe that the game belongs to the players and not to the officials. Impartial judges are needed to decide controversial issues, which are bound to come up in a game. Such judges not only prevent disputes and wrangling but they also add to the pleasure of the game.

The attitude of a good official is important. He should be confident so that there is no question about his decisions in the minds of the players. He should be willing to discuss rulings with the captain and do so in a moderated, calm manner. He should be firm but not antagonistic. Once a foul has been called, it should never be reversed unless evidence is presented to warrant reconsideration. A referee should not come down from his platform to discuss questions and interpretation.

Do not let spectators disturb the game. They will respond to a call for sportsmanship if requested to do so. The referee should leave the whistle in his mouth. It should be ready for action the instant a foul occurs. Some officials shift the whistle from side to side, indicating which team is serving the ball; others shift a towel from side to side. A favorite system is to shift an elastic band from hand to hand. It is important that the referee have some plan to aid him in keeping account of the serving side.

A referee should watch play closely as the game gets under way. It is important that his decisions be clear cut. He can use whistle signals to help him conduct the game. Two short blasts for a violation, a single blast to resume play, or a long whistle for a time-out.

On the change of serve, he should give the defensive team a reasonable amount of time to get into position. Foot faults on the serve need special attention by the referee, as the attention of the linesmen occasionally stray. The referee will also carefully check the positions of players in the screen formations to see that there is no overlapping.

STARTING THE GAME. Prior to the start of the game, the referee should inspect all equipment. He should measure the height of the net (8 feet at the center), its tautness, and the vertical markers on the side of the net, to be sure that they are directly over the side lines of the court. He should check to see that the scoring and timing devices and score sheets are ready for action. He should see to it that the game ball is properly inflated to the required pressure and that there are extra balls on hand in case of need. A good referee will check with other officials to be sure that they understand their assignments. He should check on provisions for spectator control. He should see to it that team line-ups are recorded with the scorer.

To start the game, the referee calls the captains together to decide which team gets the serve or choice of courts. The referee flips a coin and the winner of the toss takes his choice of the serve or court. He makes it clear to the captains that any questions regarding decisions must come through them.

The referee mounts the platform with the game ball. He makes a final check to see that all officials are at their post and ready to start the game. He sees that players are in their respective positions, calling a foul if any of the players are out of position when the ball is served.

GENERAL PLAY AND SPECIAL PROBLEMS

Held Balls. The most controversial play in volleyball is faulty handling of the ball. The rules indicate that the ball must be clearly hit. It specifies that only when the ball visibly comes to rest at contact may an error be called. This calls for a judgment decision on the part of the official. The big problem centers around what constitutes faulty ball handling. An official must be sure that an infraction has been committed, and he must be consistent in all rulings of this nature. Officials have been encouraged to call all underhand passes with the open hand as held balls. This has forced players to use the closed fist, wrist, back of the hand, double closed fist, or forearms in the recovery of low balls. A point that lends favor to this method of recovery is that players become amazingly adept in bringing the ball up for effective play. In fact the play is much more efficient than that of the "scoopers."

The late Dr. C. H. McCloy, formerly of the University of Iowa, studied the speed of a spiked volleyball and was requested to cooperate in the study of held balls. In a letter from him dated January 16, 1952 he wrote:

We do not know what is called the coefficient of restitution of a normally inflated ball. (This means the elasticity or rebound of the ball when struck with a given force.) This will vary with different degrees of impact. In general the harder one hits the ball, the less is this coefficient of restitution. It would certainly differ for various degrees of impact with an inflated football, like a volleyball, and might differ when one struck the ball with the fist, as in spiking, or when one struck it with two hands, as in a set up or a save from the back of the court. . . .

When one hits a golf ball with a driver, the type of action picture that is taken with "flash photography" shows that the club head is intact with the ball for at least two-thirds of an inch. With a tennis ball, it is in contact at least two or three inches before a hard-hit ball leaves the frame of the racquet. The softer the ball, the harder the hit, the longer is the hand or implement in contact with the ball.

It is therefore mechanically impossible for an instantaneous stroke, for there will be an appreciable amount of time the ball sticks to the hands.

Another simpler explanation is that a ball must come to rest for an appreciable instant when its direction is changed. This tolerance of rest makes it possible to play the ball. There is considerable discussion regarding held balls on other than underhanded recoveries, such as the serve and hard-driven spikes. The general opinion today is that officials should be strict in calling held balls, but they must also be sure that an error has been committed. They should not anticipate or call a foul when they have a hazy opinion on the play.

Thrown Balls. Throwing the ball is another violation that causes much concern. Many times the set-up places the ball in such a position that the attack must reach back over his head to hit it. In so doing, there is a great tendency to stay with the ball, thereby making it necessary to literally catch hold of the ball and throw it instead of legally hitting it. At other times the attack, in avoiding a blocker or attempting to add to the effect of the attack, will carry it from one point to another and then throw it down. Thrown balls are difficult to call at times when the action is very rapid. The point that a referee should watch is just where the spiker starts his drive. Thrown balls occur when the spiker, reaching to attack, starts the attack with his fingers on the ball. Beginners are at fault, especially when they attempt to spike with a straight arm. A fairly hit ball is one in which the spiking arm and hand make a direct hit. The time element is important. Delayed action usually means a thrown ball.

Officials will grasp every occasion to officiate at tournament matches as well as practice games. Every game should be called as though it were the final game of a championship. If an official is not sure on any point, he should counsel with other officials.

Blocking Fouls. Unlimited blocking has given additional responsibilities as well as problems to the referee. This statement is made in view of the rapid development of the game with extended rallies at the net.

It is necessary that the referee work from a platform which gives him a clear view of both courts. Leaning over the net from one side places an official at a disadvantage, especially in blocking plays.

The referee should observe the action of the blockers' hands and wrists to see that they do not follow the ball over the net. Players will vary the position of their hands; some will point the fingers directly upward, others tip them backward, and some will tip them forward, which is not advisable especially if the ball is played close to the net. He should take particular notice of how close the hands are to the net. He will also secure the assistance of the umpire to note net fouls when players are jumping up or returning to the floor from blocking action.

He should sight across the net to note any infractions on going over the net. These fouls are not too difficult to spot. However, when the ball is directly over the net, both teams may play the ball legally. This situation calls for special alertness of the referee. In blocking, the hands are usually held momentarily in place, which gives the referee a chance to see if they are over the net. When more than one player participates in a block, the rules permit any of the blockers to participate in the next play, even though it would be a successive contact.

Reaching over the Net.   Close plays at the net require keen sight on the part of the referee. The attack player is difficult to watch because his hand is moving rapidly in a whipping action to smash the ball. It is not good officiating to call a double foul to cover you when you are not sure who was over the net.

When the set up is too close to the net, the attack is likely to go over the net when hitting the ball. If the referee sights along the net when attack and blocking plays are developing, he will be ready for the play when it reaches the net. Watch for the follow-through and the flexed fingers. It is well to keep an eye on players returning to the floor after net plays. The play is not completed until all players have regained their equilibrium.

The successful referee will not be a dictator but rather a guide who makes it possible for the game to be played smoothly and with the least interference.

10

Equipment

The facilities and equipment for the game of volleyball are quite simple. The game requires a limited playing area, a ball, a net and supports, a referee's platform, a score board, and a timing device. However, it is of great importance to the proper playing of the game that the ball, net, and referee's platform conform to the specifications of the rule book, for a soft ball, a sagging net, and a lack of a referee's platform reduce the play to a poor substitute for the real game.

In view of the development of volleyball and the annual review and revision of the rules, it would be well to check the current volleyball official guides for the latest information on the game.

PLAYING AREA

The official rules call for a playing surface 60 feet by 30 feet, which includes the outer edge of the boundary lines. There should be at least 20 feet of clear space above the courts, free from obstructions. The 2-inch boundary lines should be well defined in a visible color. A 2-inch center line across the center of the court, under the net, divides the court in two. Another line, called the *spiking line,* for back-field players should be drawn across each half of the court from side to side, the center of which should be 7 feet 6 inches from and parallel to the middle of the center line. There should be at least 6 feet in back of the end lines for the service areas. If space is not available for this, the serving area should extend into the court to meet the minimum 6-foot specification. For example, if there is a wall 3 feet in back of the end line of a court, the serving line will be extended 3 feet into the court and so marked. For laying out temporary lines, masking tape serves admirably. This material is easily applied and removed. Check Diagram 1, page 10, showing court boundaries.

THE BALL

The game is played with a ball made either of a rubber bladder with a 12-piece laceless leather case or a rubber case. The ball should not be less than 26 or more than 27 inches in circumference; nor should it weigh less than 9 or more than 10 ounces. The leather case should not have less than 7 or more than 8 pounds pressure, and the rubber case not less than 5 or more than 7 pounds pressure.

Caution should be taken that volleyballs are not overinflated. The additional pressure puts a strain on the fabric lining. When inflating a ball with a rubber-core valve, moisten the inflating needle with glycerine (unless instructed otherwise). Use saddle soap to clean leather balls. Vegetable or mineral oil will help to soften harsh spots on the ball. Oil should be applied in thin uniform coats. Rubber-covered balls may be cleaned with a damp rag. If the casing has oil, grease, or mud on it, use soap and warm water. Do not use cleaning solvents on a rubber-covered ball. When a ball is punctured, it should be returned to the manufacturer for repair. A patch on the surface will not heal a puncture hole in the bladder.

NET AND SUPPORTS

The official net (see Diagram 45) should be 32 feet across and 3 feet wide, and made of 4 inch square mesh of dark brown or black No. 30 cord. The

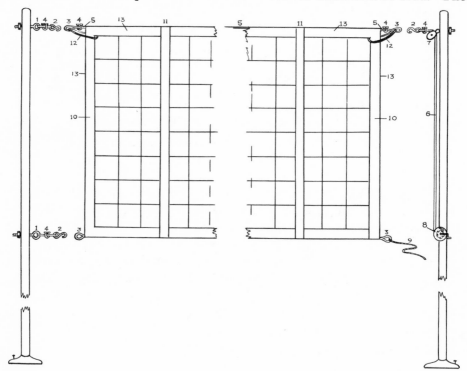

Diag. 45. Volleyball net and supports. (1) Eye. (2) S-hook. (3) Thimble. (4) U-bolt. (5) One-quarter inch flexible cable. (6) ⁵⁄₁₆-inch flexible cable. (7) Pulley. (8) Winch. (9) Rope. (10) Wooden rod (inside canvas). (11) Vertical boundary marker. (12) Tie-in. (13) 2-inch canvas.

net should be bound on all sides with a ¼-inch manila rope, and a 2-inch double thickness of white canvas sewed to the top, bottom, and sides. Through the top canvas there should run a ¼-inch preformed galvanized aircraft cable (7 by 9) with an ultimate strength of 7,000 pounds. Through the bottom of the canvas may run a ³⁄₁₆-inch cable with ultimate strength of 2,000 pounds. In addition to the above, it is advisable to insert wooden rods

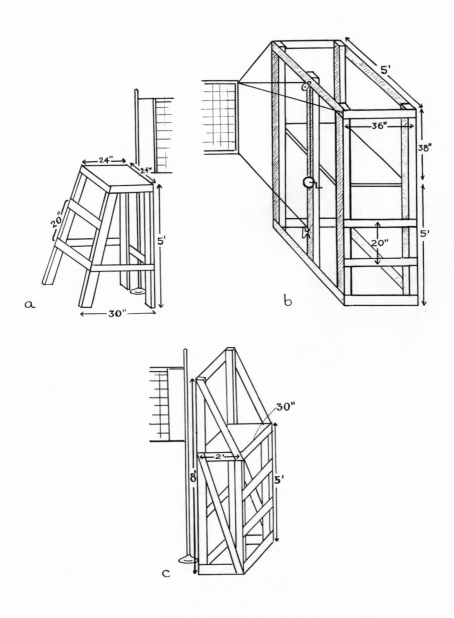

Diag. 46. Referee's platforms.

into the canvas on the sides of the net, which help to keep the net squared. A 2-inch vertical marker should be placed on the width of the net directly above the side lines. Masking or adhesive tape may be used for this purpose.

Diagram 45 shows that the top cable of the net at each corner fits around a fixture known as a metal thimble and is held in place by U-bolts. This arrangement affords an excellent attachment to tighten the net. It is also well to tie the corner rope of the net into the thimble. Metal thimbles should be installed at the lower corners of the net to protect the net. Attention to these details will save much time and effort in keeping the net in good condition, thus protecting it for extended use.

Regulation installation of the supporting post and fixtures requires a tightly stretched net between posts which are at least 3 feet and not more than 4 feet from the side lines of the court. The top of the net should be 8 feet at the center point of the court and as close as possible to this at the side lines. The galvanized cable will permit sufficient tension to hold the net in good position. A ratchet or winch must be installed on one of the posts to obtain the power needed for a tight net. To this winch a $\frac{5}{16}$-inch flexible cable is attached. This cable continues up through a pulley placed at 8 feet $1\frac{1}{2}$ inches on the post and ends in attachment to an S-hook, or halter snap, which fits into the thimble supporting the net. The cable is held in place by U-bolts that clamp the cable in a satisfactory manner.

The attachment to the opposite side of the court usually requires the use of eyebolts properly placed in relation to the style of the set-up of any particular location. The connection from these "eyes" to the net may be by cable with an S-hook that fits into the net thimble.

The rules specify that the bottom of the net should be drawn taut by ropes attached to the bottom corners of the net and then anchored into eyes or cleats on the side supports. Several manufacturing companies produce excellent supporting posts that fit into floor plates with a minimum of effort. The floor plates must be securely installed, as there is great tension from the tightly drawn cable.

Another type of installation that has been used in tournament play is a sturdy wooden fixture. This fixture may be bolted to the floor or supported by cables to withstand the strain of the net pull (see Diagram 46b).

REFEREE'S PLATFORM

The top of the supporting posts should be braced by cables attached to the wall or floor so as to permit a referee to stand and officiate the game without interference.

A convenient stand may be constructed as illustrated in Diagram 46a. Use 4-inch flooring for the top of the stand and 2 by 4-inch lumber for the legs and supports. The height of the stand is 5 feet, and the platform 24 by 24 inches. The legs are braced with 2 by 4's and the steps are 20 inches apart.

Two of the legs are slanted so as to provide steps to the platform. This angle may be secured by extending the two legs 6 inches backward from the vertical line of the back of the stand. Cross bracing, including the lower step, may be attached 20 inches from the floor. This stand can be moved with ease, and it will prove to be a valuable aid to the game.

A combination type of installation used in tournament play is a sturdy wooden fixture which is bolted to the floor (see Diagram 46b). This may be used to support the net cables as well as to provide a platform for the referee. This can be held in place with sandbags if it is preferable not to mar the floor.

This fixture is constructed with 4 by 4-inch corner posts, 8 feet 2 inches in height. A fifth 4 by 4 of the same dimension is placed in an upright position at the front center of the platform. Then a 5-foot 4 by 4 is bolted horizontally to the tops of the three front 4 by 4's. These three posts are held together at the bottom of the stand with a 2 by 4-inch timber. On one side, steps are provided 20 inches apart for convenience in mounting the platform. The latter is constructed with 4-inch flooring, supported by 2 by 4's and is 5 feet from the floor. Pulley, winch, and cable connections are attached to the center upright post. Diverging cables attached to the two front-corner posts keep the net from swaying. There is a cleat to fasten the rope from the bottom of the net.

Diagram 46c illustrates another variation. The four corner posts are 2 by 4's; the front posts are 8 feet in height and the rear posts 5 feet. These are braced by four 1 by 3-inch diagonals. The 24 by 30-inch platform is 5 feet off the floor. The bases are braced by 1 by 4's, and two 1 by 4's spaced 20 inches apart on the back of the stand facilitate mounting.

The simplest form of an official's platform is the step ladder. However, while this is a possibility, it is not a very comfortable or efficient platform from which to referee a game.

SCORING AND TIMING DEVICES

For the proper conduct of a game, there should be a combination board and timing device that is located so that it will be seen by spectators, players, coaches, officials, and others identified with the game. This board is electrically controlled by the scorer and timer. The board has two openings that flash the scores of the home and visiting teams, and a third opening gives information on the time remaining to play.

If it is not possible to secure an electrically operated board, the rules require manual scoring devices on each side of the court, and an electrical or manual timing device to time the game. A volleyball timing device is a clock that starts and stops according to the time the ball is in play. It is controlled by the timekeeper, who starts it when a serve is made and stops it the instant the ball is grounded or an official blows his whistle.

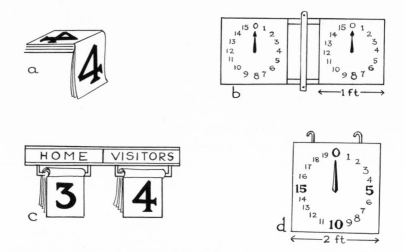

Diag. 47. Scoring devices.

For general play, simple score boards may be attached to net supports or side or end walls. These may be of the moving indicator or turnover type. The illustrations shown indicate several possibilities. These simple boards may be "home made" by "do-it-yourself" enthusiasts.

Diagram 47a is the simplest scoring device. Two sections lie on the scorer's desk. When a team scores, the scorer turns over the top leaf, which discloses the score of that team. The numbered pages are made from oil cloth, 8 by 11 inches, and are clamped to a flat board slightly larger. It is to be noted that the same score registered on the front drop faces the scorer on top of the table. The top leaf starts with a zero on top and 1 on the reverse side. This sequence will continue through to 18.

Diagram 47b has been a favorite. It is usually placed on the post at the side of the court. The player nearest to it during play keeps the score. Two 12 by 12-inch boards are painted white and connected with 2-inch strips at the top and bottom. A third strip, 2 inches wide, is nailed to the cross-supports and projects 3 inches above the support for hanging. The indicator is cut from light metal and attached to the board by means of a movable screw. The numbers 0 to 15 are painted or stenciled on the board, clockwise.

Diagram 47c is used to advantage in tournament play, as there is a place for team names to be inserted into a slot arrangement at the top of the board. The numbers are turned over on a rod fixture.

If there is a chance to hang a score board at the sides or ends of the court, Diagram 47d depicts another possibility for keeping score. A 2-foot square board, marked as shown in Diagram 47b, is supported by two iron strips bent to form hooks that fit over a rod, stall bar, or fixture. This may be installed near the server or near the net, one board for each team.

OTHER EQUIPMENT

An 8-foot measuring stick is a handy piece of equipment to have at hand for measuring the height of the net. Inasmuch as the rules call for an 8-foot net, it is good to know whether the net is "right" or not.

A volleyball score book is another essential. Both the USVBA and DGWS publish score books. Edward P. Lauten of Chicago has produced the USVBA score sheet, which contains excellent explanations. A copy of the score sheet is included in the chapter on officiating. Score books may be secured from the USVBA Printer, Berne, Indiana. The DGWS *Volleyball Guide* advertises an official volleyball score book for girls and women.

If several games are being played at the same time, officials should be sure that whistles of the same tone are not used in more than one game. Electric buzzers may be used as well as horns; confusing signals should not be used. Whistles should have strings attached to them, to go around the neck so that they will not fall. A referee generally keeps his whistle in his mouth when the ball is in play. If whistles are used by more than one person, they should be thoroughly cleaned.

MAINTENANCE AND CARE (Miscellaneous). "A stitch in time saves nine." This is most applicable to volleyball equipment. If the net has a broken cord, it should be repaired immediately. This may be done by taking a 30-inch No. 30 piece of cord and tying the center to the top section of the broken 4-inch mesh. Make a second tie 4 inches below the first tie, around the corner strings. Continue tying the string at each intersection above and below. Be sure that each tie is exactly 4 inches distant from the last tie. Tie the broken cord to the newly added string. Rips in the canvas border need to be sewn with heavy, white carpet thread. Watch for frayed ropes and replace them or repair them. Tape all frayed ropes with adhesive or masking tape; this will keep them from unraveling.

Check the floor plates to be sure that all screws and bolts are tight. Connect the standard to the floor plates and test by pulling in different directions, to see that the floor boards are not loose or sprung. Be sure that the wheel bolts on each side of the standards, which screw into the floor plates, are in place and that the pins are riveted.

Inspect the eyebolts on top of the standards and the pulley through which the supporting cable runs. This pulley should be 8 feet 2 inches from the floor. This height will permit an 8-foot net at the center point of the net. The winch or ratchet should be a heavy-duty one. Keep extra gears on hand, as those in use frequently break.

A volleyball tool and working kit should include: extra pieces of flexible cable (¼ and ⁵⁄₁₆), rope (¼ inch), masking tape, adhesive tape, No. 30 black or brown cord, an extra swivel pulley (2¼ inches), several U-bolts (1½ inches), thimbles (2½ inches), several eyebolts with nuts (1-inch diameter), an extra broom handle for the sides of the net, a small vise, pliers, screwdriver, hammer, and hack saw.

11

Volleyball for Girls and Women

Volleyball is a popular game in the curriculum of sports for women. The game has been a favorite intramural activity in elementary and secondary schools as well as in colleges and recreation centers. The game may be played by all ages, and adaptations may be made to meet the specific needs of any group.

At the present time two different organizations govern volleyball play for girls and women, namely, the Division for Girls and Women's Sports of the American Association for Health, Physical Education, and Recreation (DGWS) and the United States Volleyball Association (USVBA). Both these bodies formulate rules and publish separate volleyball guides which include these rules. The USVBA rules for girls and women are the same as for boys and men, with the single exception of the height of the net. The DGWS 1959–61 *Guide* includes an "Official" set of rules for girls and women which are comparable with but differ slightly from the USVBA rules. In addition, the DGWS *Guide* suggests modifications of the official rules for less skilled or younger players, which favor the continuance of the eight-player team, double hit, and serve assist.

Although the general trend is in the direction of the official rules, the modified game will be given consideration in this chapter in view of the number of younger and less highly skilled players. The main difference in the rules are as follows:

1. A serve may be assisted by another player.
2. In handling the ball, a player may make a second contact.
3. There are eight players, arranged three in front, two in the center, and three in back.
4. Rotation is optional.
5. Additional serve if ball hits net and goes over.
6. The game is played in two 15-minute halves.
7. The serve is made within 10 feet of the right-rear corner of the court from in back of the end line.
8. The ball must be played with hands and forearms only.
9. Limited switching of players.

GENERAL PRINCIPLES OF PLAY (MODIFIED RULES)

It is generally accepted today that the basic fundamentals of playing the ball in the women's game are similar to those of the men's game; therefore the techniques as discussed in the earlier chapters apply to women as well as men.

The serve is the same with the exception of the assist. The handling of the ball is the same when a single contact is made; however, a player may make a second contact, hitting the ball to a team mate or over the net. Many women players use the double-underhand method of receiving and passing low balls. This play has been allowed over the years. However, in many areas a stricter ruling is being made in keeping with the current official rules. It is good practice to use the head-pass technique to handle as many balls as possible. It is also suggested that teachers and coaches instruct beginners how to use the "dig" pass in recovering the ball.

Players spike the ball as in the men's game. The approach should be made from an angle or directly to the net and off two feet. With two additional players, the defense has a much greater chance to recover more plays. The half-moon defensive formation should be utilized against the attack, with two players covering the back field.

HANDLING THE BALL. In receiving or stopping an oncoming ball, a player should have a good stance that permits immediate response. In passing the ball to another player, it should be kept in front of her. The height of the pass should be about 15 feet or more, high enough for the receiver to have plenty of time to get under it. It is well to play the 1–2–3 system of pass, set up, and attack.

Whenever a team follows the men's plan of organization, there is greater opportunity for teamwork and combination plays. With the nonrotation plan it would seem advisable to have a series of combination plays at the net that would permit other than the three front players to attack the ball.

DEFENSIVE PLAY. Every member of the team should play every ball to the best of her ability. With eight players on a team, the floor should be so well covered that the opposition will find it difficult to safely place a ball. The forwards should play about 5 feet back from the net. The center-line players should play across the center of the court. The center back should cover the open area between the two center-line players, and the two corner players should cover the corners, coming in about 7 feet from the end of the court. Forward players should be coached to let high balls go to the next line of defense. They should not raise their hands over their heads to play balls that ordinarily fall into the hands of the back-field players. Players should back each other up to recover misplayed balls. The special abilities of players should be utilized in building a defense. The principle of the half-moon formation, which faces into each attack, is sound and worthy of time and effort to develop. Players should always keep their hands up, ready for play when on the defense.

A one-, two-, or three-player block may be used, depending on the nature of the attack and the abilities of the defensive team. In the men's game, the block has made a great difference in weakening the offense. When the block is used, nonblocking players should be trained to cover the areas in back of and to the sides of the blockers, as well as the center and corners of the court.

OFFENSIVE PLAY. In the men's game, the screen has general acceptance as an offensive maneuver when the ball is served. Three players may be grouped in front of the server to obstruct the opponents' view of the ball. The underhand serve is the easiest and safest method when a screen is used.

The first requisite of an effective offense is a serve that is difficult to recover. Special attention should be given to the development of a deceptive service.

The next important factor is to have the ball handled properly up to the point when the attack makes the final hit. Clear-cut passes are essential. Poorly hit balls make it much more difficult for the next player to handle. The back-field pass to the forward line must be high enough for the set-up to get under it.

If the rotation plan is used and a team is made up of four pairs, then the regular 1–2–3 system may be used. If the nonrotation plan is used and the roving back is in operation (taking the place of the server), a team must work out its plays on the basis of the strength of the individual players and their ability to handle the ball. The center-line players or the forwards may act as the set-up, or an attack player may wish to set up her own play. If she does, this must be clearly understood by other players.

It is advantageous to have all players capable of spiking the ball. This keeps the other team guessing all the time as to where the ball will be hit. The attack should be varied, and best results will come when players work in pairs.

Having an opportunity to play the ball twice gives the attack a second play to get the ball in the right position for the spike. The attack must be able to hit a ball that has been set up or she must make her own set up. Team mates must be cautious not to get in her way during these plays.

Modern play calls for more than just getting the ball over the net. The attack must hit the ball with force and direct it to the least protected areas. This calls for the ability to jump into the air and hit the ball with a cut, slice, drive, or drop. At this point it is suggested that the best system of play for effective spiking is to have the set-up place the ball for the attack to smash, rather than for the attack to set it up and then hit it. This system gives the spiker a better opportunity to concentrate on the attack.

THE OFFICIAL VOLLEYBALL RULES
(GIRLS AND WOMEN)

Advance in the style and nature of volleyball has been spearheaded through the influence of national and world tournaments. The first Open Women's Championship in the United States was held in 1949. Since that time there has been an increasing interest in competitive volleyball for women. In 1955 the USVBA adopted the same rules for women as for men, with the single exception of the height of the net (men 8 ft., women 7 ft. 6 in.—revised in 1960 to 7 ft. 4¼ in.). Along with this development, the DGWS has also changed their rules for girls and women to match the USVBA rules, with the following main differences: return to the game twice; must be in own area when ball is served; the ball is dead if it touches any part of body except hands and forearms, and a follow-through over the net is permitted with limitations.

It is to be noted, however, that researchers in the field of women's volleyball indicate that there is but limited, comprehensive written material about modern-day intensive volleyball for women in the United States and that there is a definite need for such, with special attention given to tactics and systems of play.

The United States Volleyball Association has given attention to the development of competitive volleyball for women. The *International Volleyball Review,* the *Annual Guide,* the Women's Championships as well as participation in the Pan-American games have created unusual interest. In the USVBA 1960 official *Guide,* the following comment was made regarding the 1959 Women's Championships: "The over-head or head pass was stressed with but occasional use of the under-hand pass; the set ups continue to be high and close to the net; the serves increased in deceptiveness with floaters and spins; the screen was used to some extent and the two-player block was favored. Play was characterized by friendliness and good sportsmanship."

In the following material the game as played under the USVBA rules will be used.

DIFFERENCES IN THE MEN'S AND WOMEN'S PLAY. The main difference in play at the present time is in the power attack and blocking. In general the play is slower and not so daring or so forceful. This situation can be compared to tennis, where the same factors are in operation. However, with greater experience and better conditioning to match the style of game as played by Europeans, developments are bound to take place to make the game more exciting.

Teachers and coaches in our schools and colleges will need to become familiar with the new six-player team, eliminating the assist on the serve, and double contact. Progress has been made during the past ten years in the Women's National Championships, where the rules have been the same

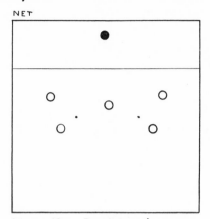

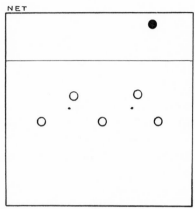

Diag. 48a. Receiving the serve (set-up in center position).

Diag. 48b. Receiving the serve (set-up in right-forward position).

as the men's. Plays that were once thought of as being impossible for women are now accepted in regular play. The defensive play of women in tournaments has been spectacular; their determination to recover plays and their zest is outstanding. They have been weaker in blocking, using the single or two-player block in preference to the three-player block.

Coaches should drill their teams in systems of play, utilizing charts, blackboard, and actual placement on the floor. Special attention should be given to positions when practice games are in session. Players should concentrate on learning their places in these plays.

RECEIVING SERVES. In Diagram 48a, set-up in the center-forward position, the set-up stays close to the net. The other five players are staggered across the center of the court. The back-field players should guard against being too far back; they should be at least 10 feet or more from the back line. Balls that go over their heads are usually out, and a lobbed ball can be easily recovered from the corners or back of the court. In Diagram 48b the set-up is in the right-forward position, and the ball should be passed to her, near the net.

In receiving the serve, players must be sure who is to play the ball when it is placed between them. If the ball is served to the right side of the court, the ball is played by the person on the right; if to the left side, by the player on the left. This gives them a better opportunity to play into the court. However, once a person has made a start for the ball, she should continue the play.

SYSTEMS OF PLAY

Two–Four. This system calls for two spikers and four set-ups. It is to be used only when attack players are not available. It is the least desirable, in view of the limited attack power, because only one spiker is in the front line at any one time, which gives the opposition too great a chance to set up its blocking defense.

Three—Three. This calls for three spikers and three set-ups. This has been the standard system of play for many years. Until recently, switching positions was not permitted, so that plays were definitely limited. In the women's rules the principle of changing positions was also restricted. However, recent changes now make many plays possible. In teaching the game to beginners, it is recommended that the 3–3 system be adopted until the players have mastered the basic skills and formations; namely, the 1–2–3 system of the pass, set up, and attack. In Diagram 2, page 12, note the position of the set-up player and her corresponding spiker. When a ball is served or played over the net, it is passed forward to the set-up in the center-forward area. In Diagram 3, page 12, the ball is passed to the set-up in the right-forward position.

When the set-up is in the center position, she may set the ball for the right forward instead of the left forward. This play is an aid to the offensive play. Another play is for the set-up to switch with the right forward and set the ball up for her. The other players move into positions to cover the field and back up the spiker to recover a returned ball. Anticipating plays and getting into position is a prime requisite of all players.

In this system there are three offensive units (set-up and attack), all working together as a team. Recoveries and teamwork help to build morale and improve playing efficiency. Each set-up should endeavor to supply the kind of a set up that her attack desires. With constant practice and team experience, a team builds a sense of unity that makes it a winning combination.

Taller players have an advantage over shorter players because greater reach enables them to spike over the block. In addition, a taller player has an advantage in blocking. Shorter players find an important position in being able to set the ball up for a perfect kill, for without a good set up, the attack will never be able to make a satisfactory spike.

Four-Two. This calls for four spikers and two set-ups. Four capable spikers are needed for this favored system of play. In the men's game this system has been accepted as the most efficient for defensive and offensive play. In the women's game it has also been recognized as a style of play that can be used with assurance of success by women and older girls. It is advisable, as recommended before, for a team of novices to start with the 3–3 system, and when the fundamental skills have been mastered and the players cooperate in basic team play, then and only then should a team switch to the 4–2 formation. If the team members are not able to use this formation efficiently and effectively, they should not continue to use it. Players may have difficulty in making the switch as well as not being able to properly cover the floor for defensive plays. Lack of experience, insufficient information, and poor explanation may be some of the causes for inability to master the play of the 4–2 system.

In Diagram 40a, page 74, the set-up may place the ball for the attack either to the right or to the left. Both spikers should approach the net as if to spike the ball, causing the defense to be uncertain where the attack will be made. If the spike is to the left of the court, the right-front player moves in; the set-up, after playing the ball, moves backward in readiness for the recovery of a blocked ball. The left back comes forward to cover the spiker, and the center back plays deep to cover the open back area. The right back moves toward the midcourt, helping to form a ring defense.

A general principle of play to be introduced at this point is that when switches are made in the forward part of the court, the set-up always switches in front of and closer to the net than the spiker.

The two set-up players carry responsibility for guiding the team in the formation and execution of plays. It is important to have a simple system of signals or calls to indicate how and where the play should be made and also to indicate weaknesses of opponents.

In Diagram 40b, page 75, the set-up is in the forward position. After the ball is served, she switches positions with the center forward so as to set the ball up for the attack, either to the right or to the left. Note that the set-up moves to the right in front of the attack. In Diagram 40c, page 75, the set-up is in the left-forward position and makes a switch to the center position.

Five–One. This system includes five spikers and one set-up. This style of play is gaining in favor in view of the potential power of having five attack players. It also makes possible greater blocking efficiency, due to the ability to add height to the block. The big problem comes in training players to carry out two different functions; namely, at one time to act as a set-up and another time as a spiker. This system is an advanced style of play, but when a group develops to a high efficiency, there is no reason why this system should not be used. It permits many opportunities for deceptive play, for quick power plays, and for placement shots.

All the spikers at the net should be alert to receive the ball for the set up. With three spikers at the net, it is possible to keep most of the attack plays in the corners, shifting to the center at times to keep the defense in a quandary as to where the ball will be spiked. The use of the low set up and quick spike can be effective.

Players in the back field may also set the first ball up to the front line for a smash on the second hit. A low arched ball may be set to the corners and can be sliced across the court.

The set-up should switch to the front line from the back court even after the serve. During this play, the center and right backs shift to the left and cover the back court. When the set-up shifts from the right-back position, all shifts are in the opposite direction.

In Diagram 49a, the set-up is playing the left-back position. She comes to the net between the left-forward and the center-forward player. She could also move into the center of the court between the center forward and the right forward, setting to attack players on either side. One weakness in this system shows up when the set-up is playing the back field and the serve is sent to her. She should be protected then as much as possible by other players.

In Diagram 49b, the set-up switches into the center-forward position, and the play is the same as for the 4–2 system. In the 5–1 system, all players must be top-level ball handlers.

Six–0. All players spike. Such a combination working together should make a formidable aggregation. It is seldom used by women's teams, but it has unlimited opportunities for excellent offensive and defensive play. Every player must be highly skilled in handling the ball and ready to go into action on the attack. Two-play formations, quick and deceptive spiking, and high effective blocking should make this system an enviable target for coaches and teams. Creative imagination makes any play possible in this system. Time will prove its effectiveness. Experimentation to date has not given sufficient returns to warrant its general acceptance.

GENERAL CONSIDERATIONS

Physical and Mental Conditioning. Physical and mental conditioning deserve the serious consideration of teachers and coaches. Special attention should be given to strengthening the fingers, hands, wrists, arms, and legs.

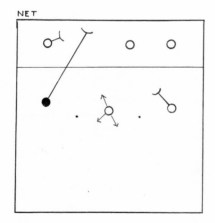

Diag. 49a. The 5–1 system (set-up in left-back position).

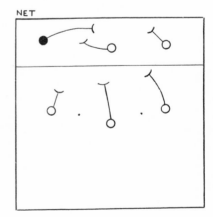

Diag. 49b. The 5–1 system (set-up in left-forward position).

Knee pads will not only protect the knees but will also make it possible for a greater number of recoveries.

Placing the Serve.   Placement of the serve and the development of serves which curve, float, wobble, or drop are of growing importance.   There is no limit as to what can be done in this skill by women.   Some players get a floater with a type of punch serve.   The hand is brought to the shoulder and punches or hits the ball just above the shoulder height.   Some use the open hand, slightly cupped.   The overhand serve is the most popular method used in competition.   Another popular serve used by women is holding the ball high overhead with the left hand and then hitting it off the hand with the right hand.

First Pass.   The importance of the first pass should be conveyed to all players.   Each player should be in readiness to play the ball when it comes to her.   The head pass should be used in as many instances as possible, and its flight should be high.   When the ball is low, a player must "dig" it out with the closed fist, back of hand, double fist, or forearms.

Spiking.   Spiking, to be effective, must be deceptive.   It is generally agreed that the two-footed take-off is preferable to the single foot.   The best approach is from the side up to an angle of 90 degrees, in which two or three strides are taken.   A spiker should use the swing of her arms and leg drive to get into the air.   She should endeavor to hit the ball with a whiplike action in which the arm, wrist, and hand snap down on the top of the ball with power.   An attack should practice with her set-up to improve her timing.   She must learn to hit the ball from different positions and in several different ways.

Blocking and Recovery.   Blocking is essential to good play.   Highly skilled spikers should always be blocked unless the ball is back from the net.   The two-player block is favored in today's play, but greater attention should be given to additional blockers.   In making a block, the fingers should be pointed straight up or tipped back slightly.

Recovery of blocked balls is another play that deserves time and practice. Beginners should avoid the tendency to spread their arms on the block and to jump forward and into and over the net.   In the block, the ball should hit the hand and be deflected backward into the court for further play.   Players must be ready to cover the areas left by the blockers.   One player should concentrate on the area in back of the block.

12

Class Organization

The first part of this chapter will be devoted to those organizations that promote volleyball as a class or intramural activity. The greatest boon that the game has received has been the splendid work of the teacher-training agencies which have included a course in volleyball for physical education and recreation majors. The following syllabus was developed at Springfield College, Springfield, Mass., during the years the writer conducted the volleyball class program. The course included 30 hours of theory and practice.

CLASS TRAINING SYLLABUS

GENERAL PURPOSE. To provide training and coaching in the fundamentals of volleyball: ball handling, serving, attack, blocking, offensive and defensive play, and officiating.

RESOURCES. The printed materials and audio-visual aids that are available were utilized.

THE ORIGIN OF THE GAME. In this section a brief review of the history of the game was presented. Developments were noted, such as its inclusion in the program of Olympic games. Attention was called to the two distinct types of the game, the recreational and highly competitive.

ADVANTAGES OF THE GAME. A brief statement was made in regard to the values of the game and its acceptance around the world.

BASIC RULES. A list of basic rules were listed, and the entire set of rules were reviewed and discussed with the class. Opportunity for officiating was provided during the game period.

OUTLINE OF THE COURSE—THE LESSON PLAN

First, Second, and Third Periods. There were three periods in the first week (the nets were not used). During this time the following subjects were discussed:

1. Introduction to the game. *Objectives: To*
   a. Develop individual skills.

    b. Learn the rules.

    c. Learn the principles of team plays.

    d. Learn officiating techniques.

    e. Gain greater appreciation of the game.

    f. Gain insights for teaching and coaching the game.

2. History of the game.

3. Importance of the game.

4. Importance of proper ball handling, demonstration. Inefficiency of the open underhand pass.

5. The underhand serve, demonstration.

6. Activity program:

    a. Warm-up and conditioning drill each day following lecture.

    b. Fundamentals of the head pass, circle and line drills, keeping ball in the air.

    c. Second-day demonstration of the underhand serve; practice hitting the ball against the wall.

    d. During the third period, the class witnessed the filmstrip "Beginning Volleyball" and the sound movie "Play Volleyball."

Fourth Period. Discussion of equipment. (Putting up and taking down nets.) Serving drills over the net. Passing drills; emphasis on getting under the ball, facing direction of the pass, and getting the ball high in the air.

Practice game play required each team to make three plays to get the ball over the net. If the ball was hit over the net on the first or second play, that team lost a point or the serve. This three-hit rule was used for six periods. It was a big help in teaching the team game.

Fifth Period. Review general principles of play, position of set-up, and 1–2–3 play. General rules for playing the game, scoring, calling your own net fouls.

Warm up; emphasis on legs, arms, and fingers. Serving practice, heel of hand. Passing practice, pass from back field to the front-center man. Let the set-up call for the ball. Three-hit rule game.

Sixth Period. Conduct the Brady test; 1 minute (see page 28). Conduct the following underhand serving test:

    Five trials into left-half of the court.

    Five trials into the right-half of the court.

    Three-hit rule game.

Seventh Period. Demonstration of general 3–3 system of play, rotation, working in pairs, the pass, set up, and attack, using six members of the class as a demonstration group. Discussion of violation of pushing or throwing the ball, due to faulty action (set up in back of spiker or use of the straight arm).

Principles of setting up the ball. Set-up players to have marked shirts. Three-hit rule game.

Eighth Period. Demonstration of getting ball off the net. Drills. Demonstration of the attack, angle of approach, two-foot take-off, jump, body and arm action, returning to the floor.

Warm-up, using approach, jump, and arm action. Drills: Hitting the ball off one hand. Jumping and hitting the ball. Bouncing ball to wall and hitting it. Having ball tossed at the net (7-foot height) and hitting it. Selection of group into teams; line up according to height; number off according to number of teams desired; let each team select a name. Play together for three periods. Play the three-hit rule game.

Ninth Period. Review fundamentals of the pass and the set up. Emphasize their importance. Demonstration of 3–3 system, working in pairs. Emphasis on team play, "three hits." Passing and serving practice.

Demonstration of the atttack, whip arm action. Attack drills; start with a low net. Play three-hit rule game.

Tenth Period. Introduce and demonstrate the use of the screen. This period is the same as the ninth period except for the use of the regular rules. Have extra players officiate; call "held balls" for all open underhand recoveries.

Eleventh Period. Underhand-serving test:

Five trials to the left-back area.

Five trials to the right-back area.

Demonstration of the overhand serve. Baseball throwing action; use of the heel of the hand. Practice overhand serving action. Serving and passing drills. Choose teams for "round robin" play. (To avoid embarrassment of the less favored players, it is well not to choose all the players. If you plan on having four teams, select players up to the point of the last remaining eight players. Instead of choosing these players, the teacher will have the eight count off in "fours," which will send two players to each of the teams. If there are three teams, the last six will be divided in this manner. This will save the unfortunate situation where the last one or two are "marked men." If the teams selected for play are unequal, it will be well to stop play at the end of the first round; otherwise two rounds make a good schedule.

Twelfth Period. Demonstration of the block. Blocking drills. Practice getting ball off the net. Overhand serving practice. Spiking drills. Team game.

Thirteenth to Thirtieth Period. Complete review of the rules, page by page, from the rule book. Warm-up each day after rule discussion. Practice serving, passing, and spiking.

The program for each class will vary in relation to special needs and weaknesses. Some classes will quickly learn the fundamental skills and be capable of advancing much swifter than other classes where faulty ball handling and careless play is in evidence. Such differences will call for special attention to various phases of the game. Much depends on the attitude of the class and its desire to learn to play the game correctly.

Tests. Repeat the Brady test in the fourteenth and twenty-eighth sessions. Give the overhand serving test in the fifteenth and twenty-ninth sessions:

> Five trials into the left-half of the court.
> Five trials into the right-half of the court.

In the thirtieth period give the following examination:

> 50 true-false questions on rules.
> 25 true-false questions on principles of play.
> 5 essay questions.

The syllabus also contained an illustrated, detailed chart of a volleyball net and supports, as well as a sample score sheet.

CLASS PLAY

PREPARING PLAYERS FOR CLASS PLAY. A good teacher or instructor will be concerned about the abilities and understanding that a novice has regarding the game of volleyball. He will also be interested in seeing to it that a beginner learns the fundamentals of play and the techniques necessary to enjoy the game. The average player is desirous of gaining skill and making progress. Satisfactions accrue when he sees improvement in his play and acceptance by other players. On the contrary, if one senses slow progress and is annoyed by other players calling attention to his faults, he is likely to develop a negative attitude toward the game. A teacher should not permit a beginner to start playing volleyball without preliminary explanation of the game, rules, and instruction in the fundamental techniques.

The teacher or volleyball leader should make an appointment with a novice and explain the general principles of play to him. This could be done by having him observe a game in progress. He should note the serve, the recovery of the serve by the receiving team and the manner in which it is passed forward to the player who sets the ball up for the spiker. He should note how the players rotate and how the score is kept. After 5 or 10 minutes of observation, the beginner should then be coached on the techniques of passing the ball. When he has learned the first steps in this skill, the teacher will teach him how to serve the ball. After this, and only then, should a beginner be introduced into an actual game. When he gets into play, it must be with a sympathetic understanding of the players who endeavor to encourage him, rather than to take the play away from him. It would be well if the novice returned for several periods for preliminary practice and study of the rules and system of play, or joined a beginners' volleyball coaching class.

CLASSIFYING PLAYERS. The first and simplest method is for the class teacher to rate the players according to their ability. A second method is to select a number of players from the class and have them classify the players. A third way is to have the class members indicate their opinions of other players in the class, listing as number 1 the player whom they think rates the highest. The fourth, and far better method, is to have the class members take several tests, such as the Brady, serving tests and others selected from those listed in the front of the book. These tests will be of greater value if retests are made, as the results will show progress and furnish incentives for improvement.

Players may be divided for class play or teams, with the better players playing on one court and the others in a second or third court. A class committee may also make up teams for play, these being posted prior to scheduled play. Another method of team selection is to designate captains and have them choose members for their teams. Consideration should be given to the feelings of the last players to be chosen. Finally, the class teacher selects the captains and members of teams. Knowing the abilities and temperaments of the various players places him in a good position for this assignment. This is especially true for regular class play. Another method is to have the teams build up on the fill-in basis, i.e., as men come on the floor, either the class director or playing leader indicates which side a new player should play on.

With limited facilities and more than 12 players for one court, there are several methods of caring for the entire group. First, the extra players sit out for one game and play in the next. This is least satisfactory. A better method is to have the extra players line up in file on the side of the court near the net, the player nearest the net being the first player to go on into the game. When a player on his side makes a misplay or foul, he takes his place, the erring player going to the end of the line and gradually working his way up. The player at the head of the line makes decisions as to who is to drop out. This decision is not to be disputed. A third method is to have a player drop out after having made one full round of positions following the serve, a player at the head of the line taking his place on the court. Some systems call for a change of players every 10 minutes or other period of time. The main object is to keep as many players as possible in the game. Sitting around waiting to play is not a pleasant status.

LEAGUES AND TOURNAMENTS

Leagues and tournaments assist in maintaining the interest of players and spectators alike. These events are the extras that break the regular routine. In general they are an asset and engender enthusiasm except when players take the game too seriously.

The naming of teams for intramural play has a great deal to do with the successful operation of a schedule. Much fun and spirit center around such titles as "Smith's Wildcats," "Brown's Tigers," "Daffydills," or the "nut," "berry," or "big leagues." A bit of thinking and originality on the part of the leaders will add much to the good spirit of the competition.

Attendance can be encouraged through a promotional program, including the mailing of post cards or letters to all members, with special attention to absentees. Original drawings and comments attract attention and help to maintain interest. League standings should be posted on the bulletin board along with special notices, general volleyball information, and pictures. Novel awards are always a source of amusement and pleasure. Gilded tin-can tops with suitable inscription make good substitutes for medals, as do cans soldered together with additional attachments such as spikes, egg beaters, spoons, etc. Humorous certificates, made up for special presentation to one or two players, add to the fun at a volleyball dinner meeting. The winning team of the league could be the guests of the other teams. A program of special short talks or a volleyball movie will help to make an evening of enjoyable fellowship.

THE ROUND ROBIN. In class play, the round-robin type of tournament gives opportunity for each team to play every other team. If there are eight or more teams, it would be well to organize into two divisions, the first two teams in each division playing in the finals.

In setting up a schedule for a round-robin tournament or league, the following method of making the draw is quite simple (note that the first team, number 1, remains in the same position while the other numbers rotate in a counterclockwise direction):

First Round	Second	Third	Fourth	Fifth	Sixth	Seventh
1–8	1–7	1–6	1–5	1–4	1–3	1–2
2–7	8–6	7–5	6–4	5–3	4–2	3–8
3–6	2–5	8–4	7–3	6–2	5–8	4–7
4–5	3–4	2–3	8–2	7–8	6–7	5–6

If there should be an odd number of teams (for example, 7), the 8 becomes a "bye" and the "bye" is entered in place of number 8. The first round would be:

1–bye   2–7   3–6   4–5

ELIMINATION TOURNAMENTS. Another type of competition is the elimination tournament, which gets its name from the fact that teams are eliminated after a single defeat (single elimination) or following a second defeat (double elimination.)

Another type is the consolation tournament, usually held in large tournaments of the single-elimination type. In this, teams that lose the first match arrange a tournament of their own and declare their champion.

The double elimination type of drawing gives a team a "second chance." A single loss does not eliminate a team from the possibility of winning the tournament. In the drawing, it is important to cross brackets to prevent pairing in the loser's bracket the same contestants who previously met in the winner's bracket.

The drawings for any tournament are important. Usually the best teams are seeded; that is, they are placed as far apart as possible. The highest rated is placed in the top position in the winners' bracket and the next best in the bottom position. If there are two teams from the same state or locality, they are placed in opposite brackets. If there is a shortage of teams to fill the schedule, it will be necessary to draw "byes." These are divided in the upper and lower brackets and spread as far as possible.

ORGANIZING AND CONDUCTING A TOURNAMENT. The following suggestions will be helpful in organizing a local or major tournament. For a single day's play using two courts, it will be possible to complete an eight-team, double-elimination tournament. With greater numbers, many modern tournaments have been divided into two divisions, each division playing a round-robin series of games. The two top teams in each division play a double-elimination tournament to declare the winner. It is not advisable to have too many teams unless there are unlimited playing facilities. Tournament directors must be ready to make adjustments in the schedule when a team or teams fail to arrive. However, schedules must be prepared and mailed to participants in advance. One of the problems of tournament play is keeping up with a time schedule. Unnecessary delays will slow up play and lower morale of players and spectators alike. Tournament directors should be sure that affected teams are informed of any adjustments in the schedule.

A sucessful tournament calls for the organization of a loyal group of volleyball enthusiasts who are willing to give time, effort, and financial support in the preparation for and the conduct of such an event. It is necessary that committees meet prior to the tournament and prepare to care for the details of their assignment.

Index

Attack, 44-56, 82
  arm and body action, 49
  drills, 52, 53
  fundamental movements, 45-49
  jump attack from stand, 45-46, 48
  running attack, 48-49
  tests, 53-56
  variations, 50-52, 75, 77

Ball, 103-4
Beginners' volleyball, 9
Berne Witness Co., 5, 109
Blocking, 59-65, 105-6
Brady test, 26, 28, 123

Championships
  Brooklyn (1922), 5
  Pan-American, 6
Class organization, 120-26
  class play, 123-24
  leagues and tournaments, 124-25
  teaching beginners, 123
  training syllabus, 120-23
Classifying players, 124
Coach, 78-81
Conditioning, 44, 82-83
Court dimensions, 9, 10, 102

Defensive play, 57-68
  blocking, 59-65
  drills, 67-68
  formations, 65
  general principles, 58-59
  half-moon defense, 67
  readiness, 57
Dig pass, 14-15
Double underhand pass, 16
Division for Girls and Women's Sports
  (DGWS), 109, 111
Drills
  attack, 52-53
  blocking, 59, 65
  defense, 67-68
  handling the ball, 24-27
  offense, 77-78
  serving, 41
Equipment, 103-10
  ball, 103-4
  maintenance, 109-10

  net and supports, 104-6
  playing area, 103
  referee's platform, 106-7
  scoring, 107-8
  timing, 107

Fundamentals of the game, 8, 11, 85

Half-moon defense, 67
Handling the ball (passing), 13-30
  beginners' weaknesses, 19, 20
  dig pass, 14-15
  double underhand pass, 16
  head pass, 17-21
  kick pass, 16
  one-hand pass, 14
  playing low balls, 14
  practice suggestions, 24-27
  Russian pass, 15
  tests, 27-30
    Brady, 26, 28, 123
  two-hand pass, 15
Head Pass, 17-21
Held balls, 100-101

International Volleyball Federation, 6
International Volleyball Review, 6

Kick pass, 16

Linesmen, 94

"Mintonette," 3

National Athletic Federation, 5
National Collegiate Athletic Association, 5
Net, 8, 104-5
  playing the ball off net, 71
  set up, 21-24
  supports, 104-6

Offensive play, 69-78
  ball off net, 71
  drills, 77-78
  fundamentals, 69
  placement of the serve, 71-72
  screen, 70, 78
  serve, 70, 71
  systems of play, 72-77

Officiating, 91-102
  hints, 99-100
  linesmen, 94
  referee, 91
  rules, 96-97
  scorer, 93
  score sheet, 92
  signals, 97
  special problems, 100-102
  terms, 94-95
  timer, 93-94
  umpire, 91

Olympic games, 6
One-hand pass, 14
Overhand serves, 35-39

Pan-American Games, 6
Passes; *see* Handling the ball
Placement
  of the attack, 54
  of the pass, 23
  of the serve, 39-40
Power volleyball, 8, 79-90
  attack, 82
  conditioning, 81
  practice game, 85-87
  pre-game considerations, 88
  schedules, 89
  scouting, 87, 88
  selection of players, 81-82
  selection of system, 84
  set-up player, 81
  teamwork, 83-84, 88-89

Referee, 11, 91
  referee's platform, 106-7
Rotation, 10
Rules, 1, 4-5, 9, 11, 96-97
  calling own fouls, 79
  terms, 95-96
  women's
    DGWS, 109, 112
    USVBA, 11, 109, 114
Russian pass, 15

Schedules, 89-90
Scoring, 10
  score sheet, 92
Scouting, 87-88
Screen, 70-71
Selection of players, 81-82
Serves, 31-43, 69-70
  curves, 33-34
  overhand, 35-39
  placement, 39-40, 71
  practice suggestions, 41

reception of, 65
rules, 31
tests, 42-43
underhand, 32-35
Set up (play), 21-24; *see also* Handling the
    Ball
  placement of, 23-24
Set-up (player), 21, 81
Spiking; *see* Attack
Springfield College, 3, 120
Syllabus, 120-23

Teamwork, 85
Terms, definitions of, 95-96
Tests, 86
  Brady, 26, 28, 123
  handling ball, 27-30
  serving, 42-43
  spiking, 53-56
  vertical jump, 53
Timekeeper, 93-94
Thrown ball, 101-2
Tournaments, 124-26
  round robin, 125
  elimination, 125-26
Two-hand pass, 15

Underhand serves, 32-35
Umpire, 91-92
U.S. Volleyball Association
  championships, 6
  formation of, 5-6
  present members, 5-6
  Volleyball Guide, 5, 91, 94, 96, 97, 109
  women's rules, 111, 114

Volleyball, 3-7
  origin of the game, 2
  first championships, 5
  power (intensive), 8, 79-90
  recreational, 8
  women's, 111-19

Women and girls' volleyball, 111-19
  blocking, 119
  defensive play, 112
  handling the ball, 112
  modified game (DGWS), 111-13
  offensive play, 113
  principles of play, 112, 114
  receiving serves, 115
  rules, 111-14
  systems of play, 115-18

Y.M.C.A., 2, 5
  Physical Directors' Society, 4